Th

You m

(

D1179395

WOLVES

THE GLORY YEARS

by

David Instone

Thomas Publications

T P

First published in Great Britain in August, 2005, by
Thomas Publications, PO Box 17, Newport,
Shropshire, England, TF10 7WT
www.thomaspublications.co.uk

ISBN 0 9512051 8 8

Printed and bound by Cromwell Press, Trowbridge

Contents

	Introduction	4
	Acknowledgements	5
1948-49:	Nearly Men No More	7
1949-50:	Pipped At The Post	17
1950-51:	A Wright Pickle	25
1951-52:	A Backward Step	34
1952-53:	On The Way Back	41
1953-54:	History Makers	48
1954-55:	A Title Thrown Away	58
	Repelling The Invaders	67
1955-56:	Challenging Again	75
1956-57:	On The Launch Pad	81
1957-58:	Champions Once More	91
	Of Wolves and England	105
	The Golden Wolf Cubs	107
1958-59:	A Victorious Defence	110
1959-60:	So Close To The Double	118
	As Time Rolled By	136
	Subscribers' Scroll of Honour	142

Introduction

This publication has been due now for close on 50 years. There have been many worthy books about Wolverhampton Wanderers, including two in recent seasons about their ground-breaking 1953-54 League Championship triumph. But never has there been a definitive hard-back tribute to the extended period of true Molineux greatness from 1949 to 1960.

They were the halcyon days when Wolves won three League titles and two FA Cups in 12 years, as well as being Championship runners-up three times. In the same period, the club's name was beamed across the world via a host of memorable floodlit nights as, chronologically, they finished sixth, second, 14th, 16th, third, first, second, third, sixth, first, first and second in the top flight.

They were the team the rest had to beat if they wanted to win anything - and they surprised even their manager. "I never imagined I would be involved in so much success," Stan Cullis said in a 1992 interview. "When I first took over, I would have been content with half-way in the League. I had to endure the arrows that were hurled at me for our so-called long-ball game but it was a bit naughty to suggest we were a kick-and-rush side because we had players in the England team for so many years."

Cullis could forgive lack of ability but not lack of application. "It's no good getting on to players about their technique if they don't have technical ability," he added. "All I ask is that they play to the best of their ability. It's the ones who think 75 per cent is good enough who leave me with room for criticism." That's why there was a notice above the Molineux dressing room door announcing: 'There's no substitute for hard work.'

With marvellous understatement, Brian Clough, who might have spotted some of his own bold confidence in the older man, said many years later: "Stanley is a true gentleman - but I bet he was a right bugger to deal with."

Bert Williams recalls his manager ticking off a player for laughing at the dinner table as they were served following a defeat at Newcastle. "This is no time for exuberance," he was told. And Eddie Stuart admits: "He did frighten us. After one game, he told me to go and see him on the Monday morning in his office, where he would always be sat in his swivel chair. I can't remember what it was about now but I know I didn't have any sleep that weekend.

"He would tell us not to dribble out of our own penalty area and he meant it, although he had apparently been a footballing centre-half himself. I once had a few strong words with him and told him he didn't know what he was talking about. He leaned close to me, very close, and said: 'I know more about football than anyone else in the world.'"

As the game evolved, for better or worse, Cullis found that the greatness he oversaw was no immunity against an undignified Molineux exit. It's a sign of the status he achieved that none of the headlines from the League titles or the FA Cups, nor perhaps even the epic win over Honved, had quite the impact as the one announcing his dismissal by Wolves in 1964.

I was lucky enough to meet and chat with Stan at his home near Malvern in April, 1990. I also saw him on several subsequent occasions at Molineux, as I did the ever-friendly and peerless Billy

Wright, whom I got to know much better during his four years as a Wolves director in the autumn of his wonderful life.

I had also visited the homes of Peter Broadbent, Ron Flowers, Johnny Hancocks, Jimmy Mullen, Bill Slater and Bert Williams for book-research purposes in 1990 and renewed a by now strong acquaintance with Bert during a chance meeting in Telford shopping centre several years ago. Having listened with me for 20 minutes or so to an eloquent man even then in his late 70s, my wife suggested I should take the time and trouble to archive the memories of these great men while they were still able to talk us through the glory years.

With sketchy interviews in dusty old notebooks from one or two who had sadly departed, I set about visiting Roy Swinbourne, Eddie Stuart, Malcolm Finlayson, Bill Shorthouse, Norman Deeley, Jimmy Dunn, Ted Farmer and, on the tragic day of September 11, Dennis Wilshaw. I wanted them to talk and talk about their lives and times at Wolves around half a century ago, and spent many hours in their company, listening in admiration and fascination.

I also went back to Bert, Bill and Ron and spoke by phone with other members of Stan Cullis' famous squads such as Sammy Smyth, George Showell and Barry Stobart. The result is Wolves: The Glory Years - the long overdue story of how Wolverhampton Wanderers came to rule the roost in Britain and Europe in a quite golden decade and a bit.

Acknowledgements

The author and publishers would like to express their sincere thanks to the players and other Wolverhampton Wanderers personnel, past and present, who have made this book possible.

The help of Christine Povey, Steve Gordos, Peter Creed and John Lalley in the research or finishing processes, or both, is also acknowledged, as is the work of Tony Matthews and Mike Slater, whose various publications on the club have been valuable sources of reference.

Tricia Freeman's design skills are responsible for the stirring cover.

Other titles by Thomas Publications are: The Bully Years (£8.99); Wolves: Exclusive! (£6.99); Sir Jack (£12.99); Forever Wolves (£16.99); When We Won the Cup (£15.99); Running With Wolves (£16.99).

All these books are available by writing to Thomas Publications, PO Box 17, Newport, Shropshire, TF10 7WT, by phoning 07734 440095 or by emailing info@thomaspublications.co.uk.

Thomas Publications are also this year bringing out:

Le Tissier **- a hard-back tribute to Southampton legend Matt Le Tissier.**

Forever Villa **- a collection of almost 400 exclusive Aston Villa pictures from right through the decades.**

Further information about all of the above titles can be obtained by logging on to our website, www.thomaspublications.co.uk.

1948-49

Nearly Men No More

For several years before and after the war, Wolves were a 'nearly' team. They lost in the 1939 FA Cup final, finished League runners-up that season for the second year running and were beaten in the title decider on the last day of 1946-47. All that, though, was under Major Frank Buckley and then Ted Vizard. When Stan Cullis switched from magnificent club and international centre-half to highly motivated manager, via a one-year stint as Vizard's assistant, so Wolves also bridged a big divide; the one separating spirited near misses from outright success.

There had been a glimpse of what might lie in store when they topped the Division One goal charts in 1947-48, Vizard's last season in charge. Their final placing of fifth was their lowest since they trailed home 15th in 1935-36 but they were having to absorb the departures of goal machine Dennis Westcott and England wing-half Tom Galley as well as find a replacement no 5 for Cullis.

By 1948-49, with Jimmy Dunn, Sammy Smyth, Jimmy Mullen, Johnny Hancocks and Jesse Pye all as regular marksmen, hopes were high, especially when they hammered Bolton 5-0 at Burnden Park and Huddersfield were slaughtered 7-1.

Manchester United, whom Cullis' men would see plenty of in a testing run-in, were also second best to them, as were the Portsmouth side who were destined to win the title twice in a row.

Jimmy Mullen is halted by a sliding tackle from Leslie Compton during Wolves' 3-1 defeat by Arsenal in the Highbury sun in September, 1948.

Jimmy Dunn challenges in a fixture at Everton - the club his Dad played for in the 1930s.

There was much individual success as well. Billy Wright had already been capped 15 times when he learned from a Wolverhampton bus conductress on his way home from an international in Copenhagen that he was to take over as England captain. And a few weeks later, Hancocks scored twice on his England debut, against Switzerland at Highbury.

Five-goal beatings came Wolves' way, though, at Aston Villa and Pompey, and there was an inconsistent streak to a squad strengthened in early spring by Dennis Wilshaw's emergence. He'd had a long, promising loan spell at Walsall, with 21 goals in 82 games, and sensationally announced himself on the bigger stage. His debut was on the left wing against Newcastle at Molineux but he hit a second-half hat-trick in a 3-0 victory. "That game got me into terrible bother at the college I taught at," he recalled. "I was really carpeted by the principal and almost thrown out. I had a conflict throughout my career of combining playing with teaching, and had to miss quite a few matches as a result. I don't think the idea ever sat very well with Stan Cullis, either."

Wilshaw immediately lost his place to the available-again Mullen but his goal exploits, mainly when going back in as centre-forward, became the talk of a spring that was all about the FA Cup. Wolves had hit Chesterfield for six in round three, then gone to Bramall Lane to despatch Sheffield United 3-0. Liverpool, beaten at the same stage in Wolves' journey to the 1939 final, were next up, having won two and drawn one of their previous three visits to Molineux.

The tie was a pertinent one for Scouser Jimmy Dunn, who was first spotted by a Molineux scout when playing for Liverpool schoolboys. "We lost 5-2 to Tranmere boys but I scored twice and he must have put a good word in for me with Major Buckley," he said. "I joined Wolves in November, 1942 at 17 and used to travel from Liverpool by train, picking up £1.50 a game plus expenses.

"I was given the same first name as my Dad because I was born on his birthday. He won the

FA Cup in 1933 with Everton, who had beaten West Ham in the semi-final at Molineux, so it was a big deal in our household that Wolves were facing Liverpool in the 1949 competition."

Dunn, who had netted at Bramall Lane in the previous round, along with Hancocks (2), also scored in front of a 54,983 crowd against Liverpool - an equaliser past former Wolves keeper Cyril Sidlow in a 3-1 win. "My father threw his hat in the air and never saw it again," he added. "I travelled home to Wednesfield on the bus with him afterwards and there was a postman standing on the platform with his bag over his shoulder as I prepared to get off near Amos Lane. He didn't know who I was and announced: 'Wolves will never do any good until they get rid of that Dunn.' I said: 'For your information, Dunn played a blinder and scored one of the goals.' I don't think that guy knows how close he came to death that day. My father would have killed him if I hadn't intervened."

At the time, Wolves were in a sticky League run that included an emphatic home defeat against champions Arsenal but the whiff of Wembley remained in their nostrils when they beat neighbours Albion 1-0 in the sixth round at Molineux. Mullen's shot 13 minutes into the second half decided this first meeting of the sides since the war and gave Wolves their first-ever FA Cup win over a Baggies side destined for promotion from the Second Division a few weeks later.

It was a momentous day for keeper Bert Williams, whose biggest scare came when an effort from namesake Cyril Williams was blocked on the line by Billy Wright. "I worked from the age of 14 at Thompsons Brothers, where there was a Mr Downey who begged Albion to give me a game," he recalls. "But they thought I was a bit small. Thankfully, Walsall did give me a go and, by coincidence, my debut was against the Albion A team in the Birmingham Combination at The Hawthorns.

"As a boy, I was a keen Albion supporter and my Dad said beforehand: 'Show plenty of confidence. If they have a penalty, take your cap off and throw it in the corner.'

"They did get a penalty and I threw my cap into the corner. But George Kinsell, a powerful left-back who I later faced at international level, scored with a kick that was so fierce, it would have killed me if I'd got in the way of it. They beat us 1-0. So much for me looking confident!"

Williams, a guest player

Bert Williams is covered by full-back Angus McLean as he repels this Arsenal attack at Highbury. The keeper initially favoured Albion and started his career at Walsall.

for Chelsea during the war, then turned down a permanent move from Walsall to Stamford Bridge, remaining loyal to his Black Country roots by switching to Wolves shortly afterwards for £3,500 - then a record fee for a keeper. He came to the fore in his new club's 1948-49 FA Cup run after, like his ex-Saddlers team-mate Hancocks, playing his first League game for them in a 6-1 thrashing of Arsenal at Molineux in 1946.

> **TIE WITH A DIFFERENCE**
> **So superstitious was Johnny Hancocks that he insisted on tying Billy Wright's bootlaces for him before each game in Wolves' 1948-49 FA Cup run.**

He was outstanding in the semi-final against Manchester United - and had to be. Matt Busby's line-up included Jack Rowley, who once scored eight times against Derby as a Wolves guest player in the war, and were not just FA Cup holders. They were also on their way to runners-up spot in the League for the third year running. "There were seven internationals in their side, so we must have been underdogs," Williams said. "It was one of the best United sides of all time."

On match-day morning, the 'Association Football Correspondent' of The Times made a remark that turned out to be almost prophetic, even if his accuracy as a forecaster proved well wide of the mark. "If one has read the signs correctly," he wrote, "the outcome is balanced delicately on the play of the four full-backs, Carey and Aston of Manchester, and Kelly and Pritchard of Wolverhampton.

"The odds are perhaps on the side of United for one would expect the greater experience of the Manchester pair to survive the speed and fearsome shooting of Hancocks and Mullen. Manchester will clearly keep (wingers) Delaney and Mitten in the picture as much as possible for rumour has it that the Wolverhampton backs are uncertain under pressure."

He concluded that United would reach Wembley and face Portsmouth - League champions elect and scourge of Wolves in the 1939 final. Pompey's path through the last-four stage didn't seem too taxing as they were meeting Second Division strugglers Leicester at Highbury.

In Wolves' clash at Hillsborough, Roy Pritchard was injured in a fifth minute collision with Delaney while going for Mitten's centre. With no substitutes allowed, he subsequently hobbled around on the left wing for nuisance value. Mullen switched to inside-left, Dunn to left-half and Wright to full-back. But worse was to follow. Lol Kelly was carried off on a stretcher after 65 minutes and was hobbliing badly when he reappeared.

Pritchard was eventually able to return to his original position but the impact of the setbacks was obvious. Wright had to produce what he rated one of his best performances and also described Williams' contribution as 'fantastic.'

With Bill Crook and Bill Shorthouse as heroes as well, Wolves even grabbed an 11th

Wolves' squad at London's Paddington Station well over 50 years ago.

minute lead when Allenby Chilton misjudged a back pass which Pye latched on to before squaring for Smyth to fire his fourth goal of the Cup journey. But United's enormous pressure, reflected in a corner count of 14-3, brought an equaliser mid-way through the first half, Kelly failing to reach Billy McGlen's diagonal lob and seeing Mitten flick past Williams.

Wolves were forced into their shells by all the problems and were thankful to survive both a further 45 minutes and then a demanding half an hour of extra-time, with Mullen - having played in the 1939 semi-final against Grimsby as a 16-year-old - even threatening a winner with a shot that Jack Crompton saved superbly.

Kelly and Pritchard did not recover for the replay a week later and their replacements hardly inspired confidence. Alf Crook, a reserve full-back whose younger brother Bill was well established in Cullis' line-up as a right-half, was playing his first competitive first-team game while Terry Springthorpe had not been seen at senior level since mid-September.

They could not have wished for a more pressurised setting than a Goodison Park packed to the rafters by 72,631. But no-one need have worried. They played a full part as two star-studded sides traded blow for blow. In constant drizzle, United started like a whirlwind and forced six early corners as Williams again performed wonders by saving headers from Ron Burke and Stan Pearson and then a 35-yarder by Rowley. Wolves replied through a close-range header by Smyth from Mullen's centre and two efforts against the bar by Hancocks, one of them a long-range free-kick.

Extra-time again seemed certain when Wolves broke through five minutes from the end. Pye drifted to the right to capitalise on a pass by Hancocks and cut in for an angled shot that was well kept out by Crompton. The keeper was only able to parry it, though, and Smyth followed up to head home.

Wolves were at Wembley for only the second time and were set to meet Leicester, shock 3-1 victors over Portsmouth. So much for the Times tipster!

Of the Goodison Park epic, one paper wrote about Williams having 'a tremendous game with no thought of his own safety.'

Jesse Pye, airborne in a Molineux raid in the company of Jimmy Mullen, faced an injury battle in the Wembley countdown. Then he had to hope he won the vote from Stan Cullis at the expense of the up-and-coming Dennis Wilshaw.

A tremendous view of Wembley's packed crowd at the 1949 FA Cup final.

But success came at a price. An injury meant he missed three out of the next seven First Division matches at the end of a season in which not one but two back-up keepers, Dennis Parsons and Nigel Sims, made their debuts; a possible explanation for a mixed Wembley build-up containing a 5-0 hiding at Portsmouth and then a 6-0 hammering of Sheffield United.

Right-back Kelly was declared fit for the final despite not playing since Hillsborough, only for his manager to stick with Springthorpe after the deputy's nine-game run in the side. The job of breaking the news fell to skipper Wright en route to London - and the consequences were dramatic indeed. The unlucky Kelly got off the coach, left his colleagues in mid-journey and made his way home.

"I was angry with Stan for not telling Lol a lot earlier about his line-up," recalls Jimmy Dunn. "He was a popular lad and took it badly when told he wasn't playing at Wembley. We could all sympathise with him when Billy read the side out."

As Kelly stepped off the team coach at a red traffic light in Oxford, there were warnings of recriminations from Cullis. Time healed the wounds, though, and the manager's threats were not seen through. Happily, Wolverhampton-born Kelly calmed down sufficiently to travel with his wife to watch the Wembley showpiece, even if it can't have been easy viewing.

There had been one more major selection issue. Wilshaw had responded to being dropped after his debut-day hat-trick by scoring twice against Stoke three games later. Another brace at Charlton in the following midweek started to make a compelling case for him and with Pye struggling to shake off a back problem, he underlined his claims by totalling three goals against Sheffield United and Manchester City in the last two matches before Wembley.

Pye, who also hit a hat-trick on his debut - against Arsenal in 1946 - had not played since the semi-final replay but was a leading character in the dressing room. He spoke with a slight stutter and Dunn revealed: "He used to put half a cigarette and a match in his shorts and nip straight to the toilet at half-time and at the end. He'd have a puff with the window open, then return to the rest of us! He was edgy before the final, though. He, Sammy and me were fearful of losing our places because Dennis Wilshaw had done so well."

This time, Cullis went with the senior option, which caused surprisingly little disappointment with the third party. Wilshaw was 23 and destined never to play in an FA Cup final but said: "I had

A Cup final close shave - but Second Division Leicester survive this time.

no complaints. I had been in a golden run, with the ball seeming to end in the net every time I touched it, and there was a lot of conjecture as to who would play.

"But Pye got fit and Stan did the fair thing by playing him. Although it would have been great to play at Wembley after the start I'd had in the team, Jesse was a tremendous player who had proved his worth with a lot of goals over the years. I didn't expect to play, so, deep down, I wasn't too disappointed. I sat on the bench and discovered how involved Stan became in games. By the end, my shoes were full of the shale he had scuffed up while kicking every ball!"

Leicester, 19th in Division Two, were the lowest-placed club ever to go to an FA Cup final and Williams said: "We knew we had a great chance because we played exciting football. We had two wingers, Johnny Hancocks and Jimmy Mullen, who could cross the ball as well as David Beckham, and forwards running in at pace to finish them off. It was a game we were all really looking forward to. Although there wasn't the razzmatazz around the final that there is these days, walking out at Wembley was still one of the great thrills in all of our careers."

A RISING TIDE
Wolves' triumphant FA Cup journey had public interest growing round by round. For successive matches played by the club in the 1948-49 competition, the attendances were 46,272, 49,796, 54,983, 55,648, 62,250, 72,631 and 98,920.

Dunn, for whom semi-final victory at his Dad's old stamping ground was particularly special, still recalls that Wolves' tactics were based on power, pressure and simplicity: "We would go out like hell to score the first goal and, if we got it, go like hell to add a second," he said. "If it didn't arrive, we would come with a rush again at the start of the second half and we were extra determined because of what happened in 1939."

13

Leicester's fifth-round victory over Luton had yielded 18 goals (5-5, then 5-3 in the replay) but they lost prolific inside-forward Don Revie three days before Wembley with a nose injury and had their second-choice keeper on duty in Gordon Bradley. Their patched-up side were trailing in the 13th minute when Pye headed home Hancocks' centre then, three minutes before the break, the same player made it two with a sharp turn and shot from inside the penalty area.

Pye had already justified his recall to the line-up but there were still anxious times ahead for the favourites, courtesy of a shot in off the post by Welsh international winger Mal Griffiths following a save by Williams from Ken Chisholm. If Wolves had not then had the rub of the green mid-way through the second half when Chisholm was flagged offside as he found the net from Griffiths' overhead pass, the scores would have been levelled at 2-2.

Instead, Wolves regrouped and ensured themselves the breathing space they needed with a wonderful 40-yard run past several defenders by Smyth, who finished with a shot to match. It was his sixth goal of the seven-game Cup run and his 22nd of the season in all competitions, making him leading scorer from Pye by one, with Hancocks, Mullen and Wilshaw also in double figures.

WOLVERHAMPTON WANDERERS FOOTBALL CLUB

CUP-FINAL
BANQUET

The Cafe Royal
Regent Street, London

SATURDAY, APRIL 30th, 1949,
7 p.m.

It's ours! Billy Wright has the FA Cup in his safe grip as he leads Wolves' triumphant players down the famous Wembley steps after the hand-over by Princess Elizabeth. The fact that the future Queen chose to wear a blue outfit for the day was as close as underdogs Leicester went to a whiff of success. Left: A treasured item of 1949 memorabilia that shows Wolves celebrated in style.

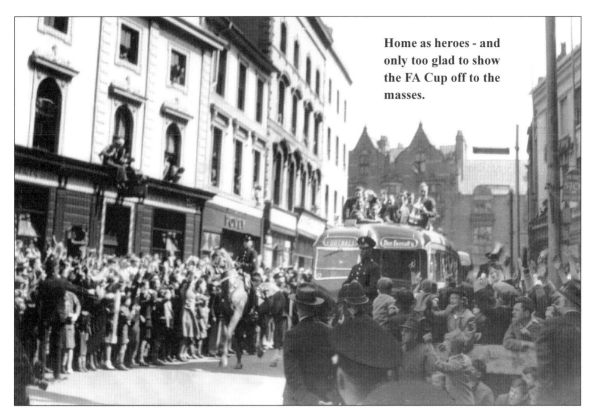

Home as heroes - and only too glad to show the FA Cup off to the masses.

"Every time I've seen my team-mates down the years, they've ribbed me about what a superb goal it was," Smyth says. "Jimmy Dunn sums it up best by saying all the Leicester defenders ran away from me. That's just about what happened. I picked the ball up in midfield, had players either side of me shouting for a pass, but saw a way to goal opening up in front of me.

"Eventually, I reached the area and got a shot away with my left which found its way into the net. Stan Cullis never let me forget it was with my left either because I didn't score many with that foot."

Dunn, who ended the season with eight goals, said: "We had that hiccup with Leicester having a goal disallowed. When I saw the ball nestling in our net, I thought: 'We're in trouble here.' But we got away with it and Sammy Smyth's goal was brilliant. I was screaming

Billy Wright cradles the Cup, with Jimmy Mullen at his side and Roy Pritchard to the right. The unlucky Lol Kelly is in the background.

for a pass but he weaved his way through and scored one of the best goals ever seen in an FA Cup final. He was always capable of that. He was a very clever player."

Smyth remains modest to the point of harbouring a slight inferiority complex as he talks of his part at the spearhead of the Cup winners' attack. He didn't sign for Wolves until he was 22, having previously worked as an electrical engineer in his native Belfast - years he believes left him with some catching up to do in the football world.

"I was not as strong as the players who had been with the club since they were 15," he added. "Nor had I got the pace of quite a few of the others but I could control the ball and pass it, and managed to score a few goals. Mind you, all you had to do in a side as talented as that was stay awake and the ball would eventually appear in front of you!"

Wright, having helped pack the kit for Wolves' 1939 final appearance and then missed seeing the game because he was representing the B team in Wolverhampton, had played for Leicester during the war. So had Mullen. They were mere side issues, though, amid the joy of Wolves being winners at last after three runners-up finishes in League and Cup shortly before the war.

It was the club's first honour since they beat Newcastle in the 1908 final at Crystal Palace and was suitably celebrated. The result was flashed out on cinemas in the town and press reports talked of women leaving their shopping to join a victory dance. Around the market, scenes were described as resembling V E Day as a line of supporters linked hands and jigged in and out of stalls. Another write-up spoke of jubilant scenes back at Wembley: "Wolves' team coach was delayed for several minutes after the game by rattle-waving fans, some of them ringing bells."

All the excitement proved too much for some as the prized silverware was passed round. Bert

More happy scenes as Bill Shorthouse, Billy Wright and Jimmy Mullen ensure that the silverware is seen by all.

Williams placed the family's Pekinese puppy in the Cup for a picture and smiles: "He peed in it. Every time now I see players drinking out of it, I can't help thinking: 'Cheers, lads!'"

1949-50

Pipped At The Post

As FA Cup holders, Wolves went to Southern Ireland in the close season, albeit with a squad considerably under-strength because of international duties. And the mood was celebratory as they showed off their prized property during a 3-2 win over a Munster Select X1 in Cork five days after a 1-1 Friday-night draw with a Bohemians Select X1 in Dublin.

Billy Wright led the group of Molineux favourites who ventured a little further afield. He won his 20th senior international cap in the game in Sweden, where a disappointing defeat led to Dennis Wilshaw's immediate promotion to the squad. "England's A and B teams were away on a combined tour of Scandinavia, with me in the B party," the forward said. "I scored two in the first B game against Finland and was switched to the A squad straightaway."

All part of the summer schedule....Wolves' players don their cricket whites at a time when they were also busy showing off the FA Cup. Among the Molineux contingent are Jimmy Mullen, Angus McLean, Sammy Smyth, Terry Springthorpe, Johnny Hancocks, Stan Cullis, Billy Wright and Bill Crook.

Above: On the slog for pre-season fitness are (left to right): Jimmy Mullen, Dougie Taft, Johnny Hancocks, Billy Wright, Terry Springthorpe, Jimmy Dunn, Sammy Smyth, Roy Pritchard and Jesse Pye. Left: Best of mates - Bert Williams, Wright and Pye.

Although he ultimately didn't get any further than watching the senior team from the sidelines, Wilshaw had the privilege of seeing club colleague Jimmy Mullen on the score-sheet in the victory in Norway five days later. It was the winger's second full cap, more than two years after his first, against Scotland, and came on the day the great Frank Swift kept goal for his country for the last time.

In turn, Swift's journey towards retirement let a third Wolves man, Bert Williams, in for an England debut the following week in a 3-1 victory in Paris that featured a rare goal by Wright. For the Molineux keeper, who had the misfortune to be beaten by Georges Moreel after only 26 seconds, international recognition was further reward for his enormous dedication against the odds.

As a youngster, he was a firm fan of Birmingham's Harry Hibbs but feared he wouldn't be big enough to fulfil his own aims of playing professionally. He was only 5ft 2in when first appearing for Walsall and was told he would have to grow six or seven inches, so he did any kind of stretching exercises he could. "I used to hang from a beam in the garage and have my brother pulling on my legs, hoping that would make me grow!" he said. "For whatever reason, I shot up to 5ft 10in and, by coincidence, it was Harry Hibbs who gave me my chance when he was Walsall manager."

Even when nature had taken its desired course, there were other obstacles barring the path of the youngster; namely, national service that meant he played some of his wartime football for Chelsea and Nottingham Forest to alleviate the difficulties of getting back to the West Midlands. "After I volunteered for the RAF and was stationed at Wing near Leighton Buzzard, I had a little Ford motor," he said. "I wrapped the engine up in cloth on Friday nights to keep it warm so I knew it would start and get me to matches.

"Another time, I couldn't get a train as planned and got a lift instead in a lorry. I had to lie on the back all the way from Lincoln to Birmingham, so I could play the next day. I couldn't leave the camp until 4.30pm or 5pm on a Friday and it was midnight when I got home. And it was mid-winter. Mind you, one of the reasons Wolves signed me was because Jack Smith, who played for Wales and was stationed with me, was appointed as trainer by Ted Vizard after the war."

With Williams safely restored, Wolves set off in 1949-50 with six straight League wins, only the last of which (3-1 at home to Middlesbrough) came by more than the odd goal. They were the only club in the country boasting such a fine record and, yet again, there was talk of them lifting the title for the first time, especially when they amazingly repeated the 7-1 thrashing they had handed out to poor Huddersfield the previous autumn.

Above: Meal-time for Wolves in the 1949-50 season, with (from left) Angus McLean, Jimmy Mullen and a young Roy Swinbourne nearest the camera. Below: Lol Kelly sees Bill Shorthouse slide in on Jack Froggatt in the drawn FA Charity Shield clash with Portsmouth at Arsenal.

Wolves, with Angus McLean happily back in action after a long absence with knee cartilage trouble, went 13 matches without defeat. The run included a 1-1 Charity Shield draw against Portsmouth in the somewhat unusual setting of a Wednesday afternoon at Highbury in the middle of October.

Wolves' goal came via

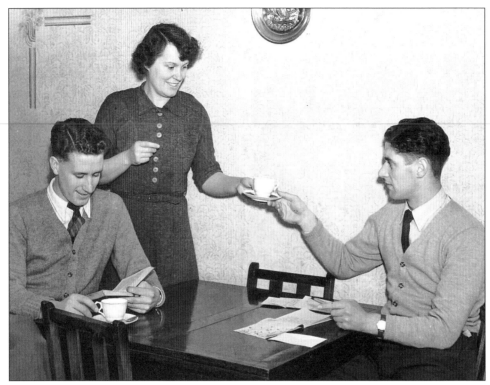

Left: Just like mother used to make it! A contented Roy Swinbourne (left) enjoys a cuppa in his digs with Jack Short. Below: Bert Williams keeps goal for England, with Scotland the opponents.

Johnny Hancocks, the side having drawn by the same score at champions Pompey in the League in the meantime to raise hopes that an even bigger prize might follow their hard-won FA Cup.

And there was delight at Molineux when Jesse Pye, even before subjecting Huddersfield to the fifth of his six hat-tricks for the club, was given a full England debut against Eire at Goodison Park. It added to his solitary victory international appearance, three B matches and one outing for the Football League representative team.

Williams kept his place against the Irish, who became the first national team from beyond British shores to win in England, Wright then being joined by Hancocks in the slaughter of Wales in mid-October. Alas, Pye's international career went no further and Hancocks had to wait another 12 months for his third and final cap. But Williams' fortunes continued to go only one way.

The former RAF high jump and sprint champion enjoyed his finest hour as an England player in front of 72,000 at White Hart Lane on November 30. With a breathtaking performance that earned him the nickname Il Gattone (The Cat) from visiting journalists, he broke Italian hearts in England's 2-0 win. The fact the goals came from Wright and Wolves' wartime star Jack Rowley underlined the immense feeling of satisfaction back at Molineux.

The keeper's sky-high standing was further consolidated a few days later when he returned to North London, this time for Wolves' game at Arsenal, and brilliantly turned a Walley Barnes penalty over the bar. He had also stopped a Derby spot-kick to guarantee maximum points at the Baseball Ground two months earlier. The side drew at Highbury but had stuttered in the meantime with successive away defeats against Manchester United, Stoke and Sunderland.

In fact, their 12th League game without defeat at the start of the season (at home to newly-promoted Albion) was also the first of 12 consecutive matches without a win - a run that inevitably cost them their place at the top. They were not helped by an injury to the Edinburgh-born Dunn, who had his sights set on winning a League title medal and Scottish caps like his father.

"Dad appeared in the 5-1 win over England at Wembley in 1928 and I crept into the running because word had got round that I was scoring a few goals for Wolves," Dunn said. "But I didn't play in 1949-50 after the November because of a back operation and, sadly, that ended my chances."

The two inside-forward positions had a less settled look than in the recent past, with Wilshaw's emergence now on a shallower curve than in the previous season, Willie Forbes in the latter stages of a promising but still unfulfilled Molineux career and Sammy Smyth managing only nine League goals in addition to his three for Ireland, including two in an 8-2 thrashing by Scotland in Belfast.

But Pye and the feared Hancocks-Mullen wing duo were still full of goals and a new young face appeared on the scene in mid-season.

Bill Crook waits for a slip from the keeper in Wolves' 2-1 win over Newcastle in 1949-50. Wolves lost at St James's on Christmas Eve.

Sammy Smyth (left) and Roy Swinbourne on the warpath as Wolves prove too strong for Blackpool at Molineux.

Roy Swinbourne, a few weeks past his 20th birthday, stopped the team's slide with two goals in a victory at Aston Villa on December 27, the very day after he had scored in a Molineux defeat against the same opponents. "It was a very exciting couple of days for me," said Swinbourne. "My father Thomas was born in Aston and had been a full-back at Villa, without getting past the reserves. I was born in Yorkshire but only because he was up there managing Denaby United at the time."

When joining Wolves at the age of 16, Swinbourne had moved into digs with Angus McLean and Roy Pritchard. The two full-backs were Bevin Boys - among the many youngsters nationwide who were conscripted by Minister of Labour Ernest Bevin to work in the coalmining industry in lieu of going in the armed services. "Angus and Roy both worked at Cannock Colliery and I remember Roy taking me out to Monmore greyhound track on my first night here," Swinbourne says.

"We lived at 86 Evans Street in Whitmore Reans with a Mrs Nuth, who was the head waitress at the Victoria Hotel in town. I later moved in with a Mrs Clark in Aldersley Avenue, Claregate, in the next road to Billy Wright, and lodged at the same house as Jack Short for a while. I was in digs for eight years before I got married, although I was in the RAF as well for a couple of years."

Another mini Wolves slump - and a somewhat unconvincing FA Cup defence - then materialised.

Despite a midweek afternoon kick-off, Wolves' FA Cup replay against Plymouth attracted a 43,835 crowd. The holders won 3-0.

No 10 Jesse Pye watches Roy Swinbourne challenge in the air during Wolves' costly game at Chelsea on April 15, 1950. The game ended 0-0 - the only one in the last five Stan Cullis' men didn't win. They obviously didn't know at the time but victory at Stamford Bridge would have made them champions.

Wolves needed two bites to remove Second Division duo Plymouth and Sheffield United, the latter after throwing away a 3-0 lead, but Blackpool, over whom Wolves had done the League double, proved one step too many as they took strides towards a Wembley visit of their own.

Wolves returned to winning ways by beating arch-rivals Pompey with a goal by makeshift centre-forward McLean - one of only two the defender mustered in 158 first-team games. Twice in the last two months, the club then won three successive League games, only for inconsistency to prevent them taking a firm grip on top spot. But Pompey at last settled into the groove of champions as they won six out of eight matches leading up to the final afternoon.

The teams were level on 51 points from 41 games but the 'for' and 'against' columns dictated that Wolves had to take more points from their last-day game against Birmingham at home than Portsmouth did against Villa.

> **SEVEN HEAVEN**
> **Huddersfield came to dread their League meetings with Wolves in the early Cullis seasons. Three times in just under three years, they were hammered 7-1 by them with Jesse Pye twice and Jimmy Dunn each scoring hat-tricks. In the odd season out, Wolves had to settle for a Christmas double over the Yorkshiremen by 2-1 and 3-1.**

Cullis' men did all they could with a 6-1 romp, going five up in the first 35 minutes despite a rare penalty miss by Hancocks. Alas, Pompey were not threatened either as they roared to an easy 5-1 victory at Fratton Park.

Wolves were only the second team to be denied the Championship on goal average - by a mere two-fifths of a goal, with Sunderland just one point back. Despite yet another near miss, though, there was much to savour. No Molineux gate had dipped below 30,000 and nine were over 50,000. The club also finished runners-up in the Central League, where Alf Crook - one of the shock heroes of the 1949 FA Cup semi-final - failed to salvage his first-team career.

Like his brother Bill, who played more than 40 senior matches in 1949-50, Crook remained a part-timer, his training confined to three nights a week. But he had fought a long battle against a knee injury that prompted Cullis to let him go. He had played only one other first-team match other than in the famous replay against Manchester United - and that in the League game at Liverpool four nights later when all his knee problems started.

Coming as he did from just down the road in Brewood and supposedly in his footballing prime at the age of 26, he was sorry to be leaving a club for whom the signs seemed good.

Stan Cullis addresses a Molineux board led by James Baker - seated at the top of the table. Also present are (from left) Charles Hunter, James Evans, James Marshall (foreground) and Arthur Oakley.

1950-51

A Wright Pickle

English football was under something of a cloud at the start of the new campaign - and those at Wolves had to accept some of the blame. Not only had the country fallen flat on their faces on their first entry into the 20-year-old World Cup competition, they had also had the embarrassment of being on the receiving end of one of the sport's biggest shocks.

Bert Williams, Billy Wright and Jimmy Mullen were all in the line-up beaten by the USA, of all sides, in the second game of their campaign in Brazil. The stunning 1-0 defeat in Belo Horizonte was sandwiched between a 2-0 win over Chile and a more acceptable second loss, this time against the hosts in Rio de Janeiro. Our World Cup was over and one newspaper hit the streets bearing a mournful black border and carrying the headline: 'Death of English Soccer.'

Mullen, having become England's first-ever used substitute - and scored - when sent on for Jackie Milburn in the pre-tournament victory in Belgium, did not play against Brazil but had a shot cleared from off the line, or maybe even behind it, against the US. And it was clear that the ignominy of losing to a side of rank outsiders as the then hopelessly inexperienced Americans were, wouldn't be overcome in a hurry.

"If we had won 10-1, it would have been a fair result," Williams says. "We hit the bar, the post, everything, but couldn't score. Then they scored from a free-kick which was going to my right before hitting someone on the knee and going in to my left. I didn't touch the ball more than six times and somehow we lost 1-0. I hated losing any match because it worried me to death. But that result really hurt and it took an awful lot of living down by all of us."

The game was Geordie-born Mullen's last

A nightmare for Bert Williams and the also-seen Billy Wright as England unbelievably lose to USA.

25

Jimmy Dunn loiters with intent near the post but Bolton clear their lines in a Molineux hammering early in 1950-51.

international for over three years and, whether or not fatigue among three such vital players was a significant factor, Wolves' campaign went downhill from a highly promising position. Their hopes were scuppered by a dreadful final seven weeks, in which they once more flirted with Wembley and saw a potential title challenge fall apart at the seams.

Things had started so brightly, with no fewer than 12 players receiving the maximum £750 benefit payments in the close season - a sign of the tendency to spend more time at one club in those days. But it was the up-and-coming Roy Swinbourne who gave the campaign exciting early impetus, heading one of the goals which beat FA Cup runners-up Liverpool on kick-off day, netting again at Fulham and hitting a hat-trick against Bolton in the annual early-season 7-1 slaughter.

Swinbourne, whose Yorkshire home had been visited several years earlier by Major Frank Buckley in the former Wolves manager's unsuccessful attempt to take him to Notts County, reached double figures in October and says: "I wasn't totally surprised because I was always ambitious and Stan Cullis put me in the side to score. If you couldn't get goals in that side, you couldn't have got them anywhere."

Despite sitting out the first four matches in the wake of his wages row, Johnny Hancocks had nine by the same juncture after a brace in a notable 4-1 triumph at Portsmouth. When the winger bagged his first hat-trick for the club to help overpower visiting Albion, Wolves had won three in a row and five out of seven, three more victories in December - one by a three-goal margin at

All dressed up and ready to travel. Wolves' players are smartly kitted out as they prepare to board their train.

A super-agile Bert Williams denies Plymouth in the FA Cup third-round tie at Home Park in January, 1951. Jack Short looks on. Wolves came out 2-1 winners.

Anfield - keeping them in the race for League honours.

But there was a degree of inconsistency, too, that had the worst spell in their skipper's career at its source. The peerless Wright suffered an injury away to Burnley in November - Wolves' second successive defeat after two consecutive victories - and missed the England v Wales friendly at Sunderland. After 37 internationals in a row, he so lost his record as the only Briton to figure in every game his country had played since the war.

For a lengthy period, Wright, who was nevertheless able to continue in Wolves' defence a week later, had grappled with his form, strangely deserted by the calming control and assurance that fans of club and country had come to take for granted. "I began to hate going on the field," he revealed. "I started to worry about what the critics would say next but knew in my heart they were right. It became a bit of an obsession with me and everything seemed to go wrong."

Maybe the strain of a World Cup finals in hotter climes had taken its toll because Mullen scored only one League goal after Christmas and Wolves went into a decline An 11-game First Division run containing eight defeats and only one win ensued and so concerned were the club that they sent Wright, who also failed his driving test at this unhappy time, off to Blackpool for a tonic, with Hancocks and Swinbourne in turn as company.

Being so close to the worldly England captain was a valuable experience for the younger Swinbourne, whose own soaraway

Williams again, this time with a penalty save from Con Martin in round four at home to Aston Villa.

progress slowed despite his braces in isolated victories against Sheffield Wednesday at Molineux and then away to Middlesbrough.

"We stayed at a place called York House," he said. "It was just a case of getting Billy away for a while from Molineux, from the press and from the other pressures but it was wonderful for me to have time in his company.

"I can't remember how many weeks we spent away from home but basically we would come back just for the matches. We'd spend the rest of the time training on the beach because it was quiet at

Wolves defend their area in numbers to repel a Huddersfield corner in the FA Cup fifth-round tie at Molineux in 1951. Bert Williams punches clear in a game won by two goals from Jimmy Dunn.

that time of year. If I remember right, we were transported there each Monday and back on the Friday in a car driven by one of the Everalls, the family who provided the team coach."

Incredibly, Wolves lost their last five home games. They didn't have it all their own way in the glory years after all then! And, as they hurtled towards a final placing of 14th - their lowest for 15 years - there was letdown, too, in the FA Cup, in which they had made steady early progress, starting with a 2-1 victory after the third-round draw had sent them on the long trip to Plymouth for the second year running.

Decisive wins followed over Villa - with the aid of a Bert Williams penalty save from his old adversary Con Martin - and Huddersfield. Then came a tough task at Sunderland, where Johnny Walker, a Scottish forward who was to total 26 goals in only 44 Wolves appearances

Roker Park joy for Wolves as they celebrate the Johnny Walker goal that earned them a quarter-final replay against Sunderland.

over five years, equalised in front of more than 62,000. The same player scored, along with Swinbourne and Dunn, to decide the replay and so earn the club a big semi-final showdown against Newcastle that became blighted by controversy.

Swinbourne laments. "We were robbed. We drew 0-0 at Hillsborough but scored what we thought was a good goal. From a chip by Billy Wright, I chested down and scored with a left-foot shot but a linesman had his flag up for offside against Johnny, although he couldn't have been interfering with play. We lost 2-1 in the replay, then Newcastle beat Blackpool in the final."

Dunn owns up to already having made a few plans for

Below: Billy Wright, Bert Williams and Bill Shorthouse rebuff an attack in the FA Cup quarter-final tie at Sunderland in February, 1951. Bottom: It's celebration time in the replay as Johnny Walker and Roy Swinbourne savour one of the goals by which Wolves won 3-1. A total of nearly 117,000 fans watched the two games.

Wembley. "My wages were something like £12 a week, with £2 win bonus, so we weren't well paid," he said. "When we were doing well in the FA Cup in 1950-51, I was keen to make some extra money. In anticipation of us reaching the final, I lined up the sale of a few tickets but we went and lost the semi-final. I realised then you should never count your chickens before they hatch."

Dunn's personal fortunes could have plummeted further shortly afterwards when he crossed swords for the only time with his manager. "I got on really well with Stan," he added. "At one stage, he thought my physique needed building up so he arranged with a local butcher, who was a Wolves supporter, to deliver 2lbs of steak to me every Friday.

"As long as Stan saw you were doing your damnedest, he would pretty much leave you alone but he couldn't stand a non-trier. He only had a go at me the once - just before the end of 1950-51 when we were playing on a hard, bouncy surface at Molineux. We had the tour of South Africa coming up a couple of weeks later and I was looking forward very much to that, so I didn't want to get injured.

"In the first half, the full-back came across from my side for a 50-50 ball and I shirked the challenge. It didn't escape Stan's attention and, at half-time, he made a bee-line for me and said: 'I know what's in your mind but if you do that again, you won't be playing for me any more.' It certainly taught me a lesson."

Jimmy Dunn, watched by Johnny Walker, is beaten by keeper Fairbrother in Wolves' unlucky defeat against Newcastle in the FA Cup semi-final replay at Huddersfield. Below: The falling Walker watches his shot dissect Joe Harvey and Fairbrother and give Wolves hope in a game which they lost 2-1.

That springtime was a chapter of opportunities missed for Wolves. Not just in the League and FA Cup, but on a personal level, especially so in the case of the Bradley-born Bill Shorthouse.

The rugged defender was led by FA officials to believe he was set for his first England call if he did a good shackling job on Jackie Milburn in the Hillsborough semi-final.

He duly did so, only still to miss out against Scotland, as he did when Bolton's Malcolm Barrass pipped him to a place in Wales the following October.

Williams, meanwhile, was an England ever-present for the season but Wright was left out of the victory over Yugoslavia (when Hancocks was in attendance) and dropped for the Festival of Britain game at home to Portugal after being recalled, with decidedly mixed results, at home to both Scotland and Argentina. The fact that his replacement Bill Nicholson scored with his first kick on his debut against Portugal briefly suggested Wright might be on dodgy ground.

But, relieved of the stresses of top-level competitive football for the first time in years, he used Wolves' trip to South Africa to rebuild his confidence. While Williams stayed at home to develop his increasing business interests and Hancocks' intense fear of flying left him with little choice but to do likewise, the skipper found the lengthy series of semi-competitive fixtures very much to his liking.

As expected, the club won all 12 of their games, scoring 60 goals in the process and conceding only five. Swinbourne hit 17 of them, including a double hat-trick (in the same game that Pye scored

> **OFF THE HOOK**
> **Roy Swinbourne, although well on the way to comfortably topping the club's appearance tally with 48 outings out of 49, was still a fresh-faced youngster when he missed the coach departing to Birmingham's New Street station for the game at Middlesbrough on April 11, 1951. In a panic, he jumped in a taxi and caught the club vehicle up on the Birmingham New Road. "We flagged the coach down and I had to walk past Stan and the directors, who always sat at the front, to take my usual seat near the back," he said. "They didn't say a word but the players made sure I knew I was in trouble." The fact that Swinbourne scored both goals in a 2-1 win at Ayresome Park - to take his season's tally to 21 - might explain why he escaped a fine!**

Roy Swinbourne takes a tumble on Wolves' tour of South Africa in the summer of 1951. But the young forward was soon back on his feet on a trip on which he ran amok. The referee, known locally as an 'umpire,' is pictured to the right, dressed in white.

Wolves on tour in South Africa. Back row (from left): Jesse Pye, Norman Deeley, Roy Pritchard, Joe Gardiner (coach), Dennis Parsons, Johnny Walker, Jack Short. Middle row: Leslie Smith, Bill Shorthouse, Bill Baxter, Roy Swinbourne, Angus McLean, Sammy Smyth, Eddie Russell, Jimmy Mullen. Front row: Stan Cullis (manager), Peter Broadbent, Charles Hunter (director), Billy Wright, James Marshall (director), Jimmy Dunn and South Africa manager Eddie Fisher.

four times) and a hat-trick. Unsubstantiated reports filtered home, suggesting Pye had been offered a deal to stay in South Africa and play for the princely sum of £1,000 a year. But subsequent events hinted that they were without real substance.

Even Cullis, four years into his retirement and a man whose only previous entry on the score sheet had been with an own goal in a record-breaking 10-1 win over Leicester in 1938, got in on the act. He rattled in a 25-yarder for the eighth of Wolves' 11 goals against South West Districts. Amid a mini injury crisis, the manager also played against Border a week later.

In between, the tourists, smitten not only by the climate but also the magnificent scenery and hospitality, found themselves up against an Eastern Province captained by Freddy Moss, a former Lower Gornal player who had emigrated to marry an African girl he had met during his war service.

Mullen had domestic matters on his mind, too, and flew home in mid-trip as his wife was expecting their second child. He experienced a scare when his plane was struck by lightning but, fortunately, it was empty at the time during a refuelling stop in Kano. And, of the first-ever South African tour by an English club, he said: "It must be the most wonderful trip any side from here has ever had in a foreign country."

More important than such platitudes, Billy Wright used the adventure to regain all his old confidence and conviction. Never again would his career touch such depths. So maybe the season hadn't been such a write-off after all. And another huge plus point had surfaced in the latter weeks of the campaign, even if Wolves supporters didn't know at the time what a terrific player new boy Peter Broadbent was to become.

South African tour of 1951

May 19 (Johannesburg): *Southern Transvaal 1 Wolves 4* (Pye, Swinbourne 2, Smyth)
May 24 (Bloemfontein): *Orange Free State and Basutoland 0 Wolves 4* (Swinbourne 2, Smyth, Walker)
May 26 (Durban): *Natal 1 Wolves 3* (Swinbourne 3)
May 31 (Pretoria): *Northern Transvaal 0 Wolves 7* (Smith, Swinbourne 2, Pye 3, Broadbent)
June 2 (Cape Town): *Western Province 0 Wolves 4* (Walker, Pye 2, Smith)
June 6 (Mossel Bay): *South West Districts 0 Wolves 11* (Walker 3, Broadbent 3, Mullen, Dunn 2, Smyth, Cullis)
June 9 (Port Elizabeth): *Eastern Province 1 Wolves 5* (Mullen, Pye, Swinbourne, Dunn, Smith)
June 13 (East London): *Border Frontier State 0 Wolves 2* (Baxter, Walker)
June 16 (Benoni): *Eastern Transvaal 0 Wolves 13* (Swinbourne 6, Pye 4, Smith 2, Wright)
June 20 (Pietermaritzburg): *Natal 1 Wolves 2* (Smyth 2)
June 23 (Durban): *South Africa 1 Wolves 4* (Smith 2, Swinbourne, Pye)
June 30 (Johannesburg): *South Africa 0 Wolves 1* (Dunn)

Joe Gardiner, a hugely liked Molineux character for many decades, is pictured in relaxed mood with Lol Kelly, Johnny Hancocks and Jesse Pye.

1951-52

A Backward Step

Peter Broadbent became England's most expensive 17-year-old when recruited in February, 1951 from Brentford for £10,000. He was recommended to Stan Cullis by George Poyser, the man who had coached the Kent-born youngster at both Griffin Park and at Dover, and who would soon be heading north himself to join the Molineux backroom staff.

Broadbent turned 18 on tour in South Africa and lodged with Poyser for a while in Whitmore Reans. But his baptism at the end of 1950-51 had hardly been happy. Despite a goal at Albion and a 'natural body swerve' his new manager believed characterised him as a truly gifted player, his first eight senior outings all ended in defeat and he was in the reserves at the start of the new campaign.

Sammy Smyth's prolific Molineux career was shortly to end with a £25,000 move to Stoke and Dennis Wilshaw and Roy Swinbourne had temporarily quietened down, so it was back to the older guard in the goal stakes.

Johnny Hancocks, who had denied reports linking him with lucrative contracts in Canada and Bogota, again scored freely following his 19 the term before, although he was unable to convince England's selectors that his international career should be extended beyond a third cap. And Jimmy Dunn's early rush of goals included a hat-trick in the rout of Huddersfield at Leeds Road.

Wolves' up-and-down start included a late-August

The colours v whites pre-season match was a well-known date on the Molineux calendar and drew crowds of many thousand. This 1951-52 version was abandoned five minutes from time because of heavy rain.

Like many up-and-coming players, Roy Swinbourne's development wasn't a constant upward curve. Pictured here hitting the bar at Manchester City, he scored only four times in the 1951-52 season.

debut for Norman Deeley, a Black Country lad whose duties used to include cleaning Bert Williams' boots. He played at right-half in a 2-1 home win over Arsenal only six weeks after appearing in the third team for the first time against Wightwick Colliery, his big day starting like so many others with the blowing-up of 24 case-balls - to be used by the first team, reserves, third team and amateur sides both for kicking-in and as spares.

Signing day for the baby-faced Norman Deeley, to the delight of Stan Cullis and club secretary Jack Howley.

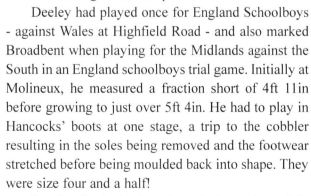

Deeley had played once for England Schoolboys - against Wales at Highfield Road - and also marked Broadbent when playing for the Midlands against the South in an England schoolboys trial game. Initially at Molineux, he measured a fraction short of 4ft 11in before growing to just over 5ft 4in. He had to play in Hancocks' boots at one stage, a trip to the cobbler resulting in the soles being removed and the footwear stretched before being moulded back into shape. They were size four and a half!

Despite Deeley's rise, through the ranks and in the physical sense, it was to be another six years before he became a first-team regular. It wasn't just his maturing as a player and the difficulties of dislodging established talented players that held him up. There was also an occupational hazard of the time - his national service. He once went a frustrating 12 months without so much as kicking a ball as Army requirements, often at Whittington Barracks near Lichfield, had to come first.

For Wolves, four successive September victories built another promising platform, then came a Pye hat-trick at home to Bolton. But a quartet of consecutive defeats, including one at champions Tottenham, followed close behind. There was also the oddity of six away score draws in a row in the League, so no wonder the side spent much of the winter bobbing around in mid-table. The impetus of those 1949 and 1950 heights was in obvious danger of being lost.

Wolves weren't helped by an injury to Williams that cost him his England place for two and a half years, for the most part to Birmingham's Gil Merrick. The keeper hurt his left shoulder diving at a Charlton player's feet in late November and the joint was almost paralysed for six weeks. He was so incapacitated during most of his three months out of the side that his wife had to dress and shave him and even comb his hair.

"I could hardly sleep," he said. "I did get back into the side well before the end of the

Ready for their pre-match meal (right) are (from the left): Peter Broadbent, Jack Short, Bill Shorthouse and Jesse Pye.

Action from one of Wolves' two mid-winter trips to Anfield in 1951-52. Len Gibbons stands firm as Dennis Parsons - in for the injured Bert Williams - gathers. Ray Chatham is the defender to the right. The clubs drew 1-1 in the League before Wolves lost 2-1 in the FA Cup a month later.

Bert Williams returned in mid-February but had no chance with this shot from Willie Moir that brought Bolton one of their goals at Burnden Park on March 1. Wolves, also represented in the picture by Len Gibbons (left) and Ray Chatham, drew 2-2 to make it eight away League games without defeat.

season but it was no good. All the time, I was conscious of my shoulder. I thought: What happens if I hit it again? It was stiff and slow, so were my reactions. Every scrap of my self-confidence had been destroyed and Stan Cullis said there was a mental barrier as much as a physical injury."

With the 32-year-old giving way first to Nigel Sims and then Dennis Parsons amid fears over his future, not even the FA Cup lifted Molineux spirits. Wolves trounced Manchester City in a replay in which John Short hinted at a permanent switch from full-back to centre-forward by scoring a brace along with Jimmy Mullen. But it was followed by a fourth-round KO at Liverpool despite another Mullen strike, and Wolves had only talent money to chase from a high League placing.

Pye stayed loyal in the face of interest from Brentford and Middlesbrough and equalised late on to salvage a draw at Bolton. But it proved to be his last but one Wolves goal and the side blew up horribly. There were shades of the previous season's collapse as they won only two of their last 14 League matches, their eight defeats including one at Old Trafford that enabled Manchester United to complete the double over them and home in on the title. Wolves' final nine games yielded only two points and their 16th-place position was two worse than 12 months earlier.

It was a trying time for Eddie Stuart to make his bow. The powerful South African, who had given up a job at Barclays Bank in Johannesburg to try his luck in England, played for the same club in his homeland as Blackpool's Bill Perry and was spotted when an ex-Bolton and England right-winger called Billy Butler went to the republic to scout for Wolves and Aston Villa.

Stuart came to be seen at Molineux as a brilliant signing - and it wasn't only at the club that he emerged as a popular arrival. "I landed in England with £50, having had a refuelling stop en route in Malta, where I bought a box of chocolates," he said. "As I settled in here, I offered one to my landlady at my digs near West Park and she took the whole lot! She was delighted with them as chocolates were still rationed in England following the war."

Stuart was to make several hundred appearances in Wolves' defence but his debut at home to Albion in mid-April was at centre-forward. The Baggies had won the Hawthorns meeting of the two clubs the previous day and prevailed again at Molineux, this time by 4-1. But Stuart had the honour of becoming Wolves' first no 9 to score in nearly four months.

He was back on the sidelines for the final home fixture of the season, against Fulham, for which the gate dipped below 20,000 for the first time since the war, then he lined up at centre-half in the last-day clash at Middlesbrough. It was a game that summed up the side's plight while also serving as an interesting reminder of the times.

Wolves players, with Eddie Stuart one in from the left, on an overnight stay in Folkestone (above left). Below: Busy in training are Johnny Hancocks, Sammy Smyth, Ken Rowley, Jesse Pye, Roy Swinbourne and Jimmy Mullen.

An early 1950s picture of Wolves' players at leisure on their travels; not that their 1951-52 adventures left them with too much to be content about.

Norman Deeley had played only five first-team games to date, none of them in the right-wing role that came to be seen as his specialist position, but Cullis was adamant in wanting him as his inside-right at Ayresome Park despite problems with the player's Army duties.

"Wolves wanted me to travel but I couldn't get away because I was on guard on the Friday night, two hours on, four hours off," he said. "It was decided I should go up on my own on the Saturday by taxi and train. I don't know whether Stan thought it was worth the trouble because we lost 4-0. If I remember right, Billy Wright was injured and couldn't do his normal job in the second half, so I had to mark Wilf Mannion. It was some consolation to me that Boro didn't score again."

It was nevertheless another sobering afternoon and full-back Roy Pritchard, on the sidelines for much of the second half of the season, said in a 1980s interview: "It's easy to look back at Wolves in the 1950s and assume we had non-stop success. But there were tough spells as well and this was definitely one of them. It was a transition time with some players coming towards the end and younger lads like Roy Swinbourne and Peter Broadbent setting off. The club stayed patient with Stan Cullis, though, and the rewards came in the following seasons."

Pye followed Smyth and Johnny Walker through the exit door, having top-scored with 15 to take the statistics of his Molineux career to 95 goals from 209 matches. He joined Luton for £5,000 at the end of a campaign in which wingers Hancocks and Mullen had each netted a dozen or more. The quirkiest scoring achievement of 1951-52, though, was the hat-trick by Ken Whitfield in the home win over Blackpool in December - the only League goals he ever registered for the club.

Amid the general disappointment, there was a bright spot. Billy Wright, who ended 1950-51 in despair, was named 1952 Footballer of the Year after playing 42 of Wolves' 45 matches and all eight internationals, including one in Switzerland which brought him his 43rd cap. That game saw him acknowledged as the country's most capped player, although most record books subsequently reduced the appearance tally of the former record holder, Bob Crompton, from 42 to 41.

While Wright was safely back in the groove, there were worries for his club and international colleague, Bert Williams. Although he played 12 times in Wolves' miserable run-in, he was still troubled by his shoulder and decided that only a rigorous and somewhat eccentric summer fitness programme would be sufficient to erase his doubts.

"At the end of 1951-52, I felt there was nothing for it but to retire," he said. "But my wife, who was my severest critic, told me I had several good years left, so I decided I had to break through that mental barrier. I began training alone for hours on end and ran miles, both in the daytime and in the dark. Every day, I ran over the muddiest and roughest ploughed fields that I could find, practising somersaults and headstands.

"If we had a party, I'd leave at 10.30 and run five miles, even in the rain. I'd find a spot where no-one could see me and fling myself on my injured shoulder. I'd lift weights and do everything I feared doing. On a bus, a woman asked my wife if she knew who that silly man was, running about the district for hours at a time. But it worked. I discovered I wasn't afraid any more and knew I'd be 100 per cent fit when I reported for pre-season training."

Jimmy Mullen's international career stalled in the early 1950s because of the stiff competition for a place - but a return to the England side wasn't far away. Here, he is pictured on the far right in training with (from left) Peter Harris, Jackie Sewell, Ronnie Allen and Johnny Haynes.

1952-53

On The Way Back

Bert Williams' reacquired fitness, happiness and confidence was one problem solved and he was to reclaim his senior jersey for the start of the new season, even if shorter-term troubles meant his understudy Nigel Sims would still play 13 League games. But another more serious health worry had confronted Wolves over the summer break.

As the club prepared to kick off their campaign at home to newly-promoted Cardiff, Eddie Stuart was taken ill following a trip back home to South Africa. So serious was his condition - a malaria-type tropical germ - that his mother was flown in to be at his bedside in Wolverhampton's Queen Victoria Nursing Institution as a specialist from London treated him.

Mrs Stuart was to stay in the Midlands for more than six weeks, although both she and her husband had been strongly opposed in the first place to waving off a boy who was now reported to

Billy Wright and Bert Williams - in action together for England against Scotland at Wembley and now back in harness for Wolves for the 1952-53 campaign after the keeper's return to full fitness.

41

Above: Bill Crook takes a tumble in a 3-1 home win against Bolton in Wolves' second League game of the 1952-53 campaign. On the left, Eddie Stuart, Roy Swinbourne and Norman Deeley await their turn for a bat in a change of sport.

be a mere two hours from death. "Apparently I was given no more than just the slenderest chance of survival," he now says. "I believe the illness was mastered only because of great medical skill and by the tremendous religious faith of my mother and myself. But Wolves did everything they possibly could as well."

Even as Stuart emerged from danger, the battle was only partly won, and manager Stan Cullis later said: "We didn't know whether he would ever be fit enough to play again." As it turned out, the player missed the entire 1952-53 campaign and was out for more than 12 months in total before regaining sufficient strength and resuming his career.

Meanwhile, Molineux had welcomed Ron Flowers, a blond wing-half who was to have a huge impact at the club for almost a decade and a half. Like Roy Swinbourne, he was a prize graduate from the Wath Wanderers nursery in his native Yorkshire and turned pro with Wolves on his 18th birthday in July, 1952. After travelling south ready to start work, he bumped into Peter Broadbent on a first-day walk round town and launched a friendship that has lasted more than half a century.

Even if they had known what good mates they were to become, though, they wouldn't quite have been prepared for the shock that awaited them when they were placed in the same digs in Chester Street, Whitmore Reans. They were to share a double bed with each other! "At least the experience has allowed me to remind Peter's missus, Shirley, over the years that I slept with him long before she ever did," Flowers smiles.

He was given an insight into Wolves' huge potential when over 15,000 watched a reserve game in his first few weeks, the club having won the Central League in each of the previous two years and just moved to a new training ground at Castlecroft. "When I was young, I collected Woodbine cigarette cards of players like Johnny Hancocks and Billy Wright, who was a hero of mine," he said. "When I found myself training with these guys, I couldn't believe it."

Flowers became a single-figure-handicap golfer and was a useful enough cricketer to be invited for a trial at Warwickshire - an opportunity he ultimately declined so he could take his parents to Blackpool on holiday instead. The seaside town played a further part in his early development because it was the visit of their footballers to Molineux, Matthews, Mortensen and all, that provided him with his Wanderers debut in September, 1952.

Wolves had included a double over Villa in an eight-game start blighted by only one defeat, Swinbourne scoring twice in a win over Bolton on his 23rd birthday. But a Flowers goal couldn't stop Blackpool coming and conquering 5-2. Having trailed leaders Liverpool only on goal average, Wolves were then 2-0 down to Manchester United in their next home game and another slaughter materialised, only this time it was Matt Busby's champions who caved in to a six-goal comeback.

John Taylor, a former Luton forward, looks towards goal in the 2-2 August draw away to Charlton.

Roy Swinbourne watches Peter Broadbent score from a right-wing cross in Wolves' 2-2 draw against a Holland X1 in Rotterdam in autumn, 1952. Leslie Smith missed a penalty in front of a 52,000 crowd.

That eye-opening victory brought Flowers his second appearance and there was an even newer face at left-half. With Wright away on duty with England, Cullis gave a debut to Bill Slater, a Lancashire-born PE lecturer at Birmingham University who had arrived from Brentford a few weeks earlier. He still played his football as an amateur but quickly blended in with the members of the paid ranks who were in sparkling form.

Swinbourne scored three against United and had started brilliantly, as he did in 1950-51. The treble took his tally into double figures in only the 11th match and, although off the score sheet when Wolves beat Newcastle to go top, he added another three in the space of only 20 minutes in a 7-3 romp at home to the other Manchester side in early November.

Having established a two-point cushion at the top, Wolves strangely failed to score in four games out of five, the odd one out a 3-2 win at Sheffield Wednesday on a day when there was a four-minute hold-up because of snow. Then problems flared at the other end of the pitch with the concession of five goals in three successive away matches straight after Christmas, the middle one at Preston ending their FA Cup hopes at the first hurdle.

Like Swinbourne, who would end the campaign as top scorer with 21, Dennis Wilshaw was enjoying something of a second coming. He netted 18 times, including braces against Albion, Manchester United and Portsmouth, although he had missed the opening nine fixtures of the season. The duo became friends for life and Wilshaw said: "We both had good seasons and were the two leading scorers as things started coming right for the club again."

Five wins in nine games had Molineux fans dreaming once more about a first title and there was an extended run in the side for Sims, who originally took over because of an injury suffered by Williams in mid-February. The changeover was seamless, the understudy playing well enough to retain his place for several weeks even after the senior man had returned to full fitness.

Wolves went top again in the spring, with Liverpool's challenge burned off. But they were pushed back to third over the closing stretch as Arsenal took the major prize by subjecting Preston to just the same fate that Wolves had suffered in 1949-50; missing out on the crown only on goal average.

Wolves' tally of 86 League goals was their highest for six years, although Jimmy Dunn had left for Derby County for £20,000 and Broadbent showed only glimpses of his own undoubted goal-scoring potential. In the tally were Slater's first three goals for the club - all in away games - and seven by Ron Stockin.

Another 29 had come from the wings, Jimmy Mullen getting 11 of them, including a brace in a magnificent 3-0 win at Old Trafford, and the remainder being supplied from the right. But by no means all of those came from the feared Hancocks boots.

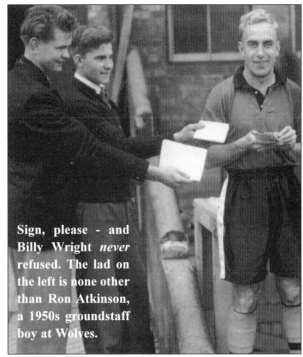

Sign, please - and Billy Wright *never* refused. The lad on the left is none other than Ron Atkinson, a 1950s groundstaff boy at Wolves.

Work-out time again, on this occasion for (from left) Bill Shorthouse, Roy Pritchard, Roy Swinbourne, Leslie Smith and Jack Short.

Stoke's goal is under threat in this attack at a sun-drenched Molineux. On the warpath yet again is Roy Swinbourne.

Stoke's penalty area is a worried place as the visitors are forced to defend in front of a packed North Bank.

Black Countryman Leslie Smith, who had first joined the club in June, 1945 as an amateur, stood in for more than a third of the season and scored eight.

With John Short and Roy Pritchard in tandem in the full-back positions for long spells, Wolves even coped well enough in the occasional absence of their skipper. Wright, who played in a 7-1 cruise for the Football League over their Irish League counterparts on home turf at Molineux, had had another excellent season with his country, rounded off by a tiring four-match summer tour of South America and North America. That excursion brought him his 50th international cap - a deserved landmark that was disappointingly marked by an odd-goal England defeat at the hands of World Cup champions Uruguay in Montevideo.

And the side's stop-off on the way home for a final game in New York gave Wright the opportunity of a fond reunion with Terry Springthorpe, one of his team-mates from Wolves' 1949 FA Cup final victory. The Shropshire-born full-back had moved to the United States via Coventry and South Africa following his departure from Molineux in 1950 and was on the

THE FAITHFUL FEW
An attendance of only 13,957 watched Wolves and Chelsea fight out a 2-2 draw at Molineux on February 18, 1953. But there was an adequate explanation. The game was played on a Wednesday afternoon.

books of New York Americans when he lined up in his adopted country's defence in their prestige friendly against England in the Big Apple in 1953.

Memories of the 1950 World Cup humiliation against the same opponents in Belo Horizonte were still relatively fresh but there was to be no upset on this occasion, England storming to a 6-3 victory under the Yankee Stadium floodlights. The game was especially arranged to mark The Queen's coronation six days earlier but was then delayed by 24 hours because of a freak rainstorm.

Wright was the only Wolves man on the tour but, with the World Cup finals in Switzerland only 12 months away, things were about to stir at Molineux in a big way. Although the club ended 1952-53 empty-handed, save for a third successive Central League title, their third-place finish in the First Division, three points adrift of the leading two, was a good riposte following mediocre placings of 14th and 16th. The pendulum had swung back in their favour and now they set about taking full advantage.

> **RESERVES REIGN AGAIN**
> Wolves thrashed Sheffield Wednesday 3-0 at Molineux to win the Central League for the third time in a row - a feat achieved in the past only by Albion (1933-35). The captain was Bill Baxter, father of Stuart Baxter, who was to be twice strongly linked with the manager's post at the club some half a century later.

Training under the watchful eye of Joe Gardiner on Molineux's perimeter track .....a tracksuited Wolves quintet with the League Championship title in their sights.

1953-54

History Makers

Four Burnley goals on the opening day, which unusually fell on a Wednesday, ensured that Wolves' 1953-54 campaign didn't immediately have the look of a title-winning year. They struck back in style, though, with Roy Swinbourne, who had scored in the first two minutes at Turf Moor, netting twice in a four-goal romp at Manchester City. The seeds were sewn.

An opening run of three successive away fixtures took another down-turn with defeat at Sunderland and, when Wolves fell behind at home to Cardiff, the omens did not appear particularly good. But a side showing a change to their forward line for the first time in 16 games, with Peter Broadbent going in for Ron Stockin, hit back to triumph 3-1 as Johnny Hancocks scored from the penalty spot for the second successive match.

Cullis' men never knew when they were beaten, their powers of recovery again surfacing when they beat visiting Sunderland despite going behind in 90 seconds. Dennis Wilshaw scored for the fourth game running and, with Bert Williams taking over from his deputy Nigel Sims, he carried the

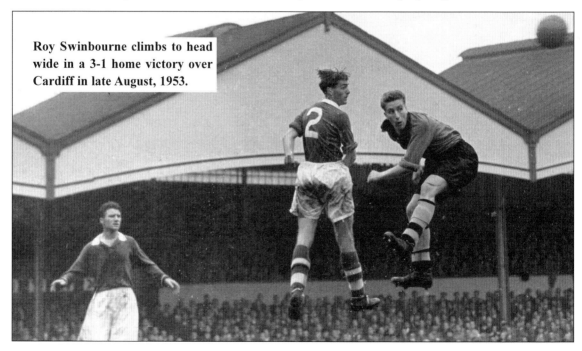

Roy Swinbourne climbs to head wide in a 3-1 home victory over Cardiff in late August, 1953.

Two magnificent views of Molineux in all its floodlit splendour during the visit of South Africa in September of 1953 - the first senior game staged at the ground under lights.

run to five matches when Johnny Hancocks' 88th minute header gave the side their first win over Arsenal at Highbury in 21 years.

The Monday evening Molineux clash with Liverpool and the visit of Portsmouth came to be regarded as yet further examples of Wolves' durability. Broadbent quickly made sure the Merseysiders' 87th minute equaliser on the first occasion counted for little, then, in a game marked by Norman Deeley's first senior outing for 17 months, Swinbourne hit the decider only three minutes from time against Pompey in a 4-3 victory that featured a second hat-trick for the club by Wilshaw - all his goals coming before half-time.

"Not many of our fans ever left games before the end," Williams recalled. "They knew we had the ability to keep going and win a match late on if we needed to. It happened much too often for it to be classed as lucky. Stan and his staff were very big on fitness and the fact that we scored so many late goals over a long period of time showed that we had the edge over a lot of teams in stamina."

Billy Wright lined up at right-back when the midweek return at Liverpool was drawn thanks to Wilshaw's ninth goal in eight matches and another northern trip, to Blackpool three days later, didn't produce a goal on a day when Bill Slater, having established himself in the side the previous spring,

Bert Williams and Roy Pritchard watch a shot flash wide in a 3-3 draw at Sheffield United.

was away on amateur international duty and Deeley was busy with forces commitments.

When Wanderers returned to Molineux, it was for an 8-1 rout of Chelsea that still ranks as the London club's heaviest defeat of all time. Hancocks was the star of the show with his second hat-trick for the club but it was an afternoon on which all five home forwards netted at least once.

Wolves stayed on the goal trail to draw at Sheffield United - their ninth successive game without defeat - before a trip to Newcastle marked them out as Championship material. Yet again they produced a late show to record their first League victory at St James' Park for almost half a century, the win being all the more worthy as Wilshaw joined Wright and Jimmy Mullen in the England line-up and made both a poignant and chequered senior debut against Wales at Cardiff.

Although the forward scored twice in a 4-1 win - he was, remember, still a teacher from Monday to Friday - a News Chronicle reporter dismissed him as not good enough to play for his country again. "I can't say I agreed," Wilshaw said almost half a century later. "Nor did my father, who went to the match. He was my biggest supporter, loved the game and travelled wherever he could to watch me play, whether it was for the Wolves first team or any of the junior sides. The fact that he witnessed me scoring twice in my first England game was very special because he died soon afterwards."

Just as Wilshaw had discovered that scoring a hat-trick on his First Division debut was not enough to keep him in

Dennis Wilshaw, the England player furthest from the camera in this photo, looks on during his international debut as Wales' Reg Davies shoots.

Photograph time for Molineux VIPS Stan Cullis, James Baker (chairman) and Jack Howley, the latter secretary for 20 years.

Wolves' line-up, so two goals in his first international didn't keep him in England's team for the 4-4 draw with the Rest of Europe in which Mullen netted twice. And his output at club level evened out as others picked up the gauntlet in a 3-1 home win over Manchester United, in tighter home victories over Preston and Albion and in clear-cut successes against Charlton and Sheffield Wednesday.

Another Hancocks penalty helped sink United despite the absence of Roy Pritchard for the first time in 1953-54, the tiny winger thus entering a destructive phase. He got the point-saver against a Bolton side defending an unbeaten home record and netted again to help bring back a point from Middlesbrough, by which time his goal tally had reached double figures.

It was a sign of Wolves' attacking riches, though, that he was still only third leading marksman - comfortably behind the side's other Ayresome Park scorers, Wilshaw (13) and Swinbourne (12). The game, the club's 14th in a row without defeat, was also the fifth in that 1953-54 season in which they had scored a vital goal in the last five minutes. There was extra significance, though, beyond the bare statistics.

Bill Slater (left) - in 1951 FA Cup final action for Blackpool.

Slater, incredibly, had been playing without pay for Wolves for over 18 months as he pursued his lecturing career, receiving only reimbursement of the half crown or so it cost him to travel on the train from Birmingham to Wolverhampton and back, and occasional kindnesses such as a festive gift from his team-mates and, when his wife was in hospital, a summons to the Cullises for his Christmas dinner!

He played on Teesside only after turning down an invitation to attend a trial match for the England amateur team - a clear sign that he was now about to join the professional ranks. "I never particularly planned to become a professional footballer," he says. "I was quite happy playing as an amateur but my head of department at Birmingham University pointed out to me that many other people working there had contracts elsewhere in various walks of life.

"He encouraged me to do the same. I played 20 or so amateur internationals for England and had trials as well, so maybe the university thought turning pro would take away those obligations. It was very strictly written into my contract that I couldn't miss lessons, so I couldn't play all midweek games, especially before floodlights came in. I also had to stay behind from some of the close-season tours Wolves had, along with the away legs in the European Cup in the late 1950s.

"I can honestly say that turning professional made very little difference to me because Stan Cullis wouldn't have tolerated anyone in his squad who wasn't fully committed anyway. The one change was that I had a second wage, which was nice, although I received less than the other players and think my highest pay from football until 1960 was £14 or £16 a week - and less in the summer."

Slater didn't turn pro until he was 26, nearly two years after playing in the 1952 Olympics. But he'd had a title-chasing team to tempt him over the threshold. Wolves were second, as they had been for much of the autumn, with Albion top following a terrific run of 28 points from 34, when the first Black Country derby of the season was contested.

Ironically, Slater missed it. This time he was with the England amateurs for a game. But, after only four minutes, Mullen - still a formidable opponent even without the blistering pace he'd been able to call on in the 1940s - did what he did in the 1949 FA Cup quarter-final clash of the clubs by scoring the only goal. The crowd of 56,590 proved to be Molineux's biggest of the season by some 11,000 and the gap was down to one point, with Huddersfield two further adrift and the rest strung out in their distant slipstream.

Wolves' win had been all the more creditable for the absence of Broadbent but he was fit for the trip to Charlton and marked it with a goal. Hancocks' strike in a comfortable win started a run of five matches in which he netted, twice in the second and last of them. Although Swinbourne also bagged a brace in the Molineux taming of Sheffield Wednesday, the winger was the club's top scorer by three at the end of his personal rush, which sandwiched one of the nation's darkest football days.

Williams, part of the debacle against the USA three and a half years earlier, was on the sidelines

this time but Wright, as ever, was present in a game that cost England their proud, long unbeaten record at home against sides from out of the home islands. The Olympic champions, Hungary,

Billy Wright smiles as he leads England into Wembley battle with Hungary. Very soon, though, the mood was much gloomier.....

on an astonishing run of 29 games without losing, exposed previously unseen flaws in the home ranks as they bewildered, tormented and outclassed Walter Winterbottom's team.

Embarrassingly, it finished 6-3, and many believed the Magyars' supremacy was even more pronounced than that. "I was stripped as a sub for the game and was absolutely sick with the result even though I didn't get on," Williams said. "I still felt it very badly."

The humiliation put domestic football under a critical light and Wolves became torch-bearers in the repair effort when they thrillingly won at Tottenham for the only time in the 1950s to finally overhaul their neighbours. It was their 18th successive match unbeaten and they had won 14 successive home games going back to the previous February. But their elation was short-lived.

When they faced Burnley at Molineux at the start of the second half of their season, they scored another late goal through Hancocks. On this occasion, though, it was mere consolation in a 2-1 defeat. The fourth-placed Clarets had done the double over them and Albion leapfrogged back to top spot by drawing at Arsenal.

The fifth successive game in which Hancocks scored was the home win over Manchester City, one of his two coming from a penalty. They led again as a result of Albion's defeat at Bolton, then slipped once more at home to Aston Villa on Christmas Eve as a side skippered by newly-transferred former Molineux man Bill Baxter hit back from behind to win.

Fortunately, they immediately gave another demonstration of their own powers of recovery in the Boxing Day return, Wilshaw heading an 88th minute winner after Hancocks had come up with a quick equaliser in the first half.

Victory at Cardiff in the first game of the new year, secured by goals from the club's three top

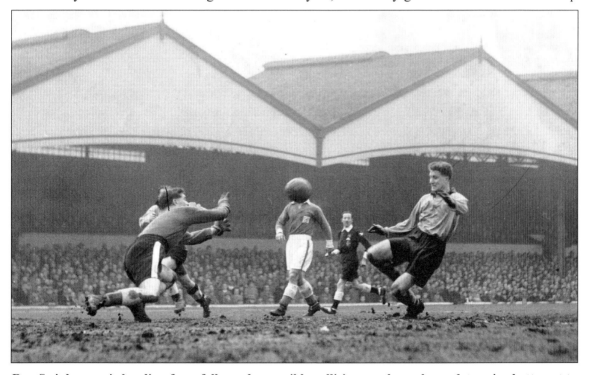

Roy Swinbourne is heading for a fall - and a possible collision - as he makes a determined attempt to reach a 50-50 ball in a game played near the mid-point of Wolves' historic 1953-54 campaign.

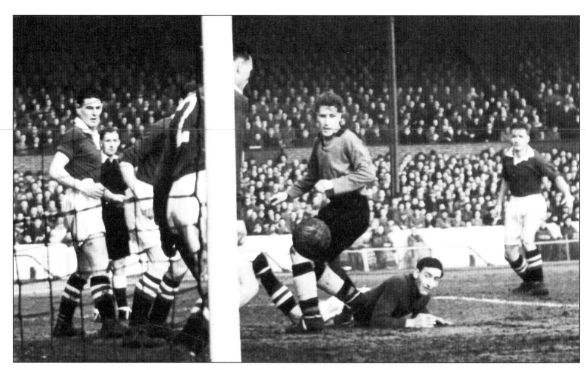

Wolves are shut out on their visit to Stamford Bridge in February, 1954 as right-back Harris clears off the line with keeper Thomson beaten. Roy Swinbourne is the attacker for a Wolves side beaten 4-2 in front of a crowd of more than 60,000. Swinbourne and Dennis Wilshaw scored their goals.

scorers, suggested Wolves were right back in the groove. Flowers' appearance at Ninian Park was only his second of the season in the senior side and he stayed in a team who then suffered three quick losses that put a big dent in their challenge.

After Second Division Birmingham produced a major shock to oust them from the FA Cup, they had Wright at centre-half for the injured Shorthouse against Arsenal as they failed to score at home for the only time in 1953-54. The Gunners rode their luck to win 2-0 after four first-half efforts had struck their bar, Broadbent then departing to Bologna to win his only England under-23 cap in what was the country's first-ever game at that level.

Even the club's brilliant form on the road deserted them at Portsmouth, where they suffered their first away defeat since August. Wilshaw did not play because he was with his dying father but he was back for the visit of Blackpool when a second-half Swinbourne hat-trick saw off the FA Cup holders. A goal at Chelsea then confirmed the centre-forward's return to scoring form, even if Wolves crashed 4-2.

Albion were three points clear with just under a third of the season left but saw the lead slashed while they were on FA Cup duty. Their rivals cashed in with a 6-1 slaughter of Sheffield United, Swinbourne and Hancocks each netting braces to stand on 21 and 22 goals respectively, with Wilshaw's strike leaving him on 21. Hancocks had set a new club record for a winger for the second time by beating his tally of 19 in 1950-51.

The game was notable for two other factors. It was Slater's first as a professional (although he remained part-time) and marked the return of Eddie Stuart following his life-threatening illness, the

South African making two of the goals against the Blades and finding it third time lucky after defeats in his first two senior appearances 22 months earlier.

Slater was knocked out when heading a dramatic late winner at home to Newcastle in late February; dramatic because the visitors had themselves scored twice in the last ten minutes to apparently save a point. Slater held a curious record that was to last until the end of the season. Having also netted at Manchester City in August, he was the only half-back or defender to score for the club throughout the 1953-54 campaign.

With Pritchard approaching the end of a Wolves career of 223 appearances, Shorthouse was having a spell in a less familiar role at left-back while his more favoured place at centre-half passed to Wright, who really wanted to play at left-half. But before the win over Newcastle, Cullis said: "Billy has been playing that well at centre-half that I just can't move him."

Wolves gave a debut to the 19-year-old Eddie Clamp at sixth-placed Manchester United, the switch of Flowers to centre-forward failing to pay off in a 1-0 defeat secured by a controversial late Johnny Berry goal. But another stand-in, Les Smith, played a full part as Mullen's replacement in the next game and set up a second-half winner for Wilshaw at FA Cup semi-finalists Preston.

Wolves failed to capitalise on Albion's 5-0 crash at Chelsea when they only drew at home to Bolton on a night when Wilshaw couldn't get away from his teaching duties and Clamp played his second and last game of the season. The Molineux crowd of only 19,617, the lowest of 1953-54, were not impressed.

The little-used Deeley was having a run at left-half but the side got worse before getting better, going 3-0 down by half-time at home to bottom-but-one Middlesbrough. They finished 4-2 losers despite a late Broadbent brace that made him the fourth Wolves player to take his goal total into double figures.

The deficit on Albion, who beat Port Vale in that day's FA Cup semi-final, was still two points, although the Baggies blew their match in hand by losing on a midweek afternoon at Sunderland, where keeper Norman Heath suffered the neck injury that prevented him playing again. The door was still open……and Wolves were at The Hawthorns the following Saturday.

A game billed as the title decider was robbed of four star attractions when England's 4-2 victory away to Scotland the same day took Wright and Mullen out of Wolves' side and Ronnie Allen and Johnny Nicholls from Albion's team. While Cullis recalled Pritchard at left-back and again switched Shorthouse across to centre-half, the Baggies were shorn of no fewer than five of their regulars and then had Ray Barlow - standing in as a centre-forward - incapacitated by an early leg injury.

It was not a great spectacle for the 55,000 crowd but Wolves were content enough after Swinbourne had turned sharply to blast in the only goal in the 58th minute. The side's first win at the ground in 19 years had completed a crucial double and put them top on goal average with five matches left.

"It was a big win because we had been neck and neck with them for so long," the match-winner said. "Albion were in with a good chance of doing the League and Cup double, so it was a good scalp for us. I've been very friendly with Ray Barlow over the years and he still talks about the kick from Bill Shorthouse that left him limping that day. Every time he sees me, he pretends to jump and asks: 'Have you brought that Shorthouse with you?'"

The follow-up was thoroughly convincing. Charlton contained two debutants on their visit to Molineux and were despatched 5-0. Hancocks, back on his favoured wing after swapping to accommodate Smith at The Hawthorns, scored twice and then missed a penalty. Mullen also hit two and the day became better

Billy Wright challenges Stan Mortensen and Bill Perry in the draw at Blackpool in 1953-54.

still with news of Albion's defeat at Cardiff. Wolves were two points clear with four game to go.

With Wright now at left-back, they drew at lowly Sheffield Wednesday while their rivals beat Manchester City. But another swing came on Easter Monday. Albion drew at home to Villa and, across the Black Country, third-in-the-table Huddersfield, ex-Molineux defender Lol Kelly and all, were crushed by goals from Mullen, Hancocks, Broadbent and Wilshaw, Hancocks also missing a penalty on a day when some reports said he scored from a free-kick from 'not far inside the Huddersfield half.'

Wolves would have had their first title wrapped up a little earlier but for the intervention of a man who was destined to become a major figure himself at Molineux. Wilshaw had levelled in the return at Huddersfield only 24 hours later when the home right-half lashed a 25-yard shot past the flailing Bert Williams. The scorer's name: Bill McGarry.

Wolves, who had been backed at Leeds Road by an estimated 8,000 supporters (their biggest following since the 1949 FA Cup semi-final) knew, courtesy of Albion's remarkable 6-1 collapse at Villa, that the title was already as good as won. They were still two points clear with a game to go - and with a vastly superior goal average to boot. Not only would they need to lose their final game at home to Tottenham to let Albion back in but the Baggies would have to win at Portsmouth and achieve a swing in their favour of something like 13 goals.

Football League officials refused to tempt fate by taking the Championship trophy to Molineux for the big day, no doubt mindful of the dramatic afternoon in 1946-47 when they had transported the silverware to Wolverhampton, only to have to pack it back off to Preston when Ted Vizard's Wanderers team - needing only a draw to be sure - lost to Liverpool in Cullis' final game as a player.

In 1954, there were no such slips. Swinbourne scored both goals in a 2-0 victory to take his haul for the season to 24. The club, who were able to field the same side in each of the final five matches, had scored the most goals in the division (96) and conceded the fewest (56) so their right to the Championship for the first time in the 65 years of the Football League could not be questioned.

It was a memorable time, not only for the older stagers like Williams, Wright, Shorthouse, Hancocks, Wilshaw, Mullen and the management duo of Cullis and Joe Gardiner, but also the newer brigade. In particular, it was a fabulous welcome-back present for Stuart, who had re-emerged from his near-death experience to play the last 12 games of the season.

Stuart's first target had been a fairly modest one: to make 12 appearances in the first team. "At that point, Stan Cullis used to say: 'Right, you can go to Burslem's now (a store in Darlington Street run by a Geoff Burslem) and be measured for your blazer.' When he said that to me, I felt ten feet tall. I would rather have had that blazer than £10,000."

The points and the title in the bag, Wolves had to wait another two weeks and two days to get their hands on the silverware. The hand-over came at a banquet at the Civic Hall on May 10, when League president Arthur Drewry praised them royally. "The team that wins this trophy is still the best team in the world," he said.

Remarkably, for an era marked by loyalty, long service and much less freedom of movement, Hancocks had become the club's only ever-present between Tom Galley in 1938-39 and Bobby Thomson in 1962-63. More importantly, Wolves were top dogs and, six years later, the football world would still be saying it.

WOLVERHAMPTON WANDERERS. F. C.1953-4
FOOTBALL LEAGUE DIVISION. I - CHAMPIONS

P. 42
W. 25
D. 7
L. 10

F. 96
A. 56
PTS. 57

R.Flowers   E.Stuart   B.Williams   J.Mullen   R.Swinbourne
W.Shorthouse   Mr.Stan Cullis   J.Gardiner   W.J.Slater
(Manager)   (Trainer)
P.Broadbent   W.Wright   League   J.Hancocks   D.Wilshaw
(Captain)   Cup

1954-55

A Title Thrown Away

Wolves' players may have departed on their summer break on a high but three of them reported for pre-season training with their colours somewhat lowered. From the joy of Molineux, Billy Wright, Dennis Wilshaw and Jimmy Mullen went off for a hectic and largely unhappy few weeks with their England international colleagues.

Wright and Mullen played in a friendly defeat in Yugoslavia in mid-May before the esteemed captain of club and country was the sole Molineux representative on an even more sobering occasion - the 7-1 spanking in Hungary. He was one of only four survivors from the Magyars' wonderful win at Wembley in the previous November, when one newspaper report had famously described his face at the end as being as white as his three-lions shirt.

It was - and still is - England's heaviest ever loss and was no sort of preparation for the World Cup finals in Switzerland a month later. The shockwaves rippled into the opening game of the tournament, a 4-4 draw with Belgium in Basle, then Mullen and Wilshaw were recalled for the second match - against the hosts in front of a bumper 60,000 audience in Berne - and came up with the goals in a 2-0 victory.

The latter clash was Wright's first start as an England centre-half, with Bill McGarry making his debut in the reshuffle that followed. Mullen found himself jettisoned, though, for the quarter-final clash with holders Uruguay in Basle, where a 4-2 defeat ended British interest. But it was West Germany and not the South Americans

Wolves' players board their flight for the pre-season game against First Vienna.

or highly fancied Hungarians, the latter unbeaten for four years, who were to lift the trophy for the first time.

Wolves did some travelling of their own despite rejecting an invitation to a tournament in Brazil as it fell too close to the start of the campaign. They drew a friendly in Austria, having flown out of Birmingham several weeks earlier - minus Bert Williams, Johnny Hancocks, Bill Slater and their current England men - for a tour of Denmark and Sweden.

Scandinavian Tour of 1954

Thursday, April 29: *Aarhus Combined X1 0 Wolves 5*
Tuesday, May 4: *Helsingborg 0 Wolves 5*
Thursday, May 6: *Copenhagen Combined X1 2 Wolves 2*

There was a poignant moment at the airport prior to departure for Scandinavia as they crossed paths with Albion keeper Norman Heath. He was still on a stretcher and Wolves' players found time to console him after his flight back to the Midlands following the career-ending neck injury suffered in the game at Sunderland during the 1953-54 championship run-in.

When the title defence got under way, Roy Swinbourne quickly returned to the groove, notching twice in an opening-day win over Sheffield Wednesday - a 4-2 scoreline Wolves repeated when gaining early revenge for a defeat at Tottenham, Spurs' Ralph Wetton scoring an own goal in both meetings. Wilshaw was also accumulating steadily and, with a couple against Sunderland, helped inspire an autumn run of four straight wins.

By then, Wright had followed his international switch to centre-half by doing the same for Wolves. Only very rarely for his club and never for his country did he play anywhere else again. Bill Shorthouse, whose head injury at Portsmouth had prompted the rethink, was sufficiently displeased about his resulting switch to full-back as to consider asking for a transfer.

Hancocks was having a slow start amid more thoughts of what-might-have-been. Like Dennis Bergkamp, he was a frightened, highly reluctant flier, the fear greatly stunting his England chances. "He has thrown away hundreds of pounds in his career by refusing to go with representative teams but we can't expect him suddenly to change," manager Stan Cullis said.

New season, same story. Wolves went into 1954-55 with a 4-2 victory. It came against a Sheffield Wednesday line-up unable to keep out this Jimmy Mullen shot. Also pictured is Roy Swinbourne - scorer of two of the other goals.

Even a coach ride to Merseyside or Yorkshire was an ordeal for him and he'd surely have been in the shake-up for Switzerland after taking his goal tally for the club to 121 in League and Cup with the 25 (only one behind Wilshaw) he contributed to the title-winning season. Not bad for a 5ft 4in winger who cost a paltry £4,000 from Walsall!

It wasn't until the home win over Manchester United in early October that Hancocks netted, Peter Broadbent also using that game to break his 1954-55 duck. The 4-2 victory kicked off a sequence of nine matches without defeat and came three days after Wolves had fought out a Charity Shield thriller with Albion. The clubs, having tossed for choice of venue, drew 4-4 at Molineux, Swinbourne scoring twice and Ronnie Allen helping himself to a hat-trick.

"There was no animosity or viciousness when we faced Albion," Bert Williams recalls. "It was never a war. Ronnie, Johnny Nicholls, Ray Barlow and Len Millard were genuine, nice people and the spirit of our matches was helped by the fact that so many of the players were local. It was Johnny Nicholls' biggest regret that he never played for Wolves."

When Albion returned to Wolverhampton in the League three weeks later, they were thrashed 4-0. And a 5-0 mauling

Images of two famous Wolves games against Albion early in 1954-55. Bill Slater, Roy Swinbourne and Dennis Wilshaw threaten (above) in a 4-0 home League victory at Molineux. The romp came a month after an epic 4-4 Charity Shield draw at the ground, the teams for which are reproduced below.

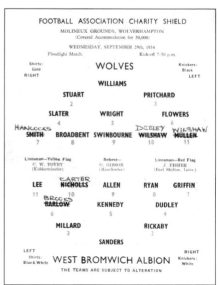

Burnley survive on this occasion during their visit to Molineux on November 6, 1954. But they were crushed 5-0 with Roy Swinbourne, pictured leading the charge here, and Ron Flowers each scoring twice.

of a Burnley side who had done the double over Cullis' men in the previous season helped take the title holders three points clear at the summit.

Four points from three games kept the pot boiling nicely and Wolves were red hot on the night they thrashed Spartak in one of the famous floodlit fixtures given a thorough airing in the next chapter.

Back on the First Division front, Chelsea halted the champions' runaway progress with a thrilling 4-3 triumph at Molineux, only for Wolves to regain their formidable autumn edge straightaway with a Hancocks brace earning two points at Leicester.

The winger, whose tiny feet packed awesome power, had become the first Wolves player since the war to hit the target in six successive first-team matches. By a major coincidence, Wilshaw then did exactly the same in the next six games, the duo unsurprisingly going on to top the club's goal charts with totals of 28 and 25 goals respectively.

"From the days when I used to fire shots at my brother on a piece of waste ground, I have practised with both feet," Hancocks said in an interview during his career. "Although I have such small feet, I can get as much power behind my shots as most players."

Wright was the only Wolves player to survive into the start of England's 1954-55 programme, the World Cup proving to be the swansong for Mullen's 12-cap career. But the captain had a different colleague for company on the grander stage when Slater added to his amateur international recognition with a debut in the paid ranks at right-half in the Wembley win over Wales in the second week of November.

The 'new boy,' well established in the same role

The slaying of Spartak at a misty, rainy Molineux.

Not this time - but Wolves roared back from two down to score three times in front of a massed South Bank and sensationally put Hungarian masters Honved to flight in December, 1954.

at First Division level, kept his place in the victory over world champions West Germany but Wolves went into a December decline - a surprise development given that it was in that month that they conquered mighty Honved. The launch of Wilshaw's run of seven goals in six games strangely coincided with the start of the rot, which included an Everton win in the last Christmas Day match staged in Wolverhampton. The festive crowd of 28,494 was the third lowest of the season.

Wobbling Wolves even needed to hit back from two down to prevail at Grimsby, from Division Three North, in the third round of the FA Cup. Five goals in the final 20 minutes prevented the trot without a win stretching to five; instead, the side turned things round superbly and reeled off four consecutive victories after Swinbourne's goal had knocked out Arsenal at Molineux in round four.

Roy Swinbourne (left) heads an FA Cup winner against Arsenal in 1955.

In a bizarre run of four League matches, Wolves then wilted 6-1 away to Bolton (where Williams left the scene injured and had to be replaced as keeper by Flowers), overpowered Huddersfield 6-4, won 4-2 in the snow at Old Trafford and hammered visiting Leicester 5-0.

Hancocks hit three against Huddersfield at Molineux and two at home to Leicester, only

The key moment in the title battle of 1954-55 (above) as Bert Williams fails to reach the 75th minute Peter Sillett penalty that went a long way to ensuring that Chelsea, not Wolves, would win the title. Right: Eric Parsons crosses as Bill Shorthouse lunges in.

for the well to run dry for the leaders when they lost at mid-table West Brom and saw Chelsea close in fast.

Five matches brought Wolves only two points, the last of them on Easter Saturday handing the title initiative to Chelsea. Ted Drake's team had come with a rush after standing 12th at the end of October, a rearranged game played in front of a meagre 7,764 gate away to Albion proving the turning point. On a snowy midweek March afternoon, they hit back spectacularly to win 4-2 after trailing with ten minutes left.

The Londoners were three points clear of Cullis' men when they welcomed them to Stamford Bridge, which was creaking under the strain of an incredible 75,000 - some 27,000 above the season's average gate! And they stretched the gap to five, Peter Sillett scoring the only goal from a 75th minute penalty conceded by Wright's diving goalkeeper-style save on the line from Seamus O'Connell. Hancocks then hit the post but the hosts held on.

Chelsea, who hadn't won in the previous seven Easters, duly celebrated their 50th anniversary with the title but their 52 points equalled the lowest ever winners' total. Wolves knew, as in 1950 and 1953, that it wouldn't have taken much more to be champions. With only eight points from their last 11 games, they finished second, four points adrift and above Portsmouth and Manchester United on goal average. What might have happened had the injured Swinbourne not missed the run-in?

Their dismal run-in also contained FA Cup disappointment. After a Wilshaw hat-trick in the space of 22 minutes had buried fancied Charlton in the Molineux snow on fifth-round day, they went down 2-0 on another wintry surface in the quarter-final at Sunderland, where they lost Shorthouse with concussion in only the fourth minute; it summed up another of their so-near-yet-so-far seasons following the ecstasy of the previous year.

The highlights of the spring were individual ones. Williams, having used the visit of West Germany to win his 19th England cap more than three years after picking up his 18th, stayed in the side for the fixture with Scotland in April and for summer matches in France, Spain and Portugal.

The Scotland and France games were red-letter occasions for two of his Molineux team-mates. Flowers' excellence over three years in Wolves' first team brought him a senior international debut in the 1-0 defeat in Paris, albeit a few weeks later than planned. "It was in the days when the England team was picked by selectors, rather than a manager or coach," he said. "We were about to play Albion in midweek prior to the England v Scotland game and the Wolves director, Mr Oakley, who was also on the FA, told me I was playing at Wembley. I'd never played there, so I was delighted. But I was caught in the face by George Lee in the derby and broke my nose. I was in hospital for about a week and it was only after I'd recovered that I was told I'd had a blood clot dangerously close to my brain."

Wilshaw did play and made history as the first (and still only) England man to score four in a game against Scotland, who thus lost at Wembley for the first time in 21 years. Duncan Edwards was hailed the same day as England's youngest full international at 18 years, 183 days. Only later was it discovered that one James Princep was 17 years 252 days when he faced Scotland in 1879.

"I had a bit of a present from the keeper in the first minute," Wilshaw admitted. "He came out too far for a Stan Matthews cross, dropped it on to my weaker right foot and I walloped it first time through the legs of a defender. It was a happy start and I added three more in fairly quick succession in the second half to round off a great day."

Despite a mid-20s club goal haul for the second season running, Wilshaw never felt completely comfortable in football and put his insecurity down to the fact that he was only part-time. "I didn't see the other players from one Saturday to the next and although that caused no problem with them because the spirit in the dressing room was so good, it was difficult trying to marry a teaching career in Hanley with my football in Wolverhampton," he said.

A newspaper image reflects Billy Wright's despair as he and his keeper, Bert Williams, are beaten by a second goal by Sunderland in the FA Cup quarter-final at Roker Park in 1955.

"I think the main trouble was that Stan hadn't got control over me full-time. I always thought that had an effect on my football and also probably affected my relationship with him. I used to think he was treating me very badly by leaving me out on occasions but I learned to appreciate over the years that I must have been a real nuisance to him. Having a first-team player whom you didn't have full control over must have been a pain.

"Whatever our differences, though, I stress I had the greatest respect for him. And he must have valued me because he made special arrangements to have me flown, after lessons, to a League game at Sunderland one night in the 1954-55 season. It was just the pilot and me in a tiny plane which didn't seem to clear the chimneys by very much! I didn't score in the game or excel in any way, so I don't know whether Stan thought it was worth all the effort."

Wilshaw was airborne with the rest of his team-mates - and on this occasion Williams and Slater travelled, too - when Wolves broke further ground with their trip to Russia early in the summer of 1955. The club's players, who flew via Helsinki, were taken to see landmarks that were

Trouble ahead for Billy Wright and Bert Williams in Wolves' game against Moscow Spartak. Below: Postcards from Russia, with Wright and Roy Swinbourne sightseeing (left) and Peter Broadbent ready for take-off (right). In the centre, a group look at the distinctive open stadium.

Above: Billy Wright at leisure. Below left: One of the programmes in Moscow - unreadable to western eyes!

No way through for Roy Swinbourne against Spartak, although he wins this header.

off limits to many westerners but the curiosity of the Kremlin, Red Square and Lenin's tomb paled against the match-day disappointment. Wolves were beaten 3-0 by Moscow Spartak and lost 3-2 to Moscow Dynamo five days later despite two goals from Wilshaw.

With Arsenal having lost 5-0 behind the Iron Curtain the previous October, there was a feeling that English football was back at square one. It was enough to prompt one gloomy commentator to describe the defeats as more demoralising than the hidings handed out at international level by Hungary. And the setbacks came after Wolves had done so much to rebuild national football pride in their own back-yard.

THE FLOODLIT ERA

Repelling The Invaders

They led to what Stan Cullis described as 'the most exciting game I have ever seen,' had his team hailed as world champions and prompted one pundit to suggest that Molineux should provide the entire England side. But the beams of light that illuminated Wolverhampton Wanderers in all their 1950s magnificence might never have been installed.

The floodlit revolution nearly didn't reach Wolverhampton, at least not in the club's pomp, because some councillors fretted over the aesthetic damage the giant pylons would do to the town skyline. Even the visionary Cullis admitted they were a gamble. But £20,000 was never better spent. Wolves were playing thrilling, winning football and now the world could see how they had the other superpowers from home and abroad chasing shadows.

The switch-on came on Wednesday, September 30 against a South African X1 on what proved a particularly memorable night for Eddie Stuart. The defender had made his comeback after illness in the annual colours v whites match at the start of the season, and a building-up of his strength in the reserves had him something like match-fit again.

Bill Shorthouse, recognising his young colleague's strong sense of patriotism, sportingly stood down and allowed him to face his countrymen in his place. More than that, Stuart was made captain for the evening and says: "It was a wonderful experience for me. I went on to play a lot of games for Wolves as skipper but that was the first time. I was incredibly proud just to play against the national team from my home country - and to lead the side out made it even more special."

Wolves v South Africa: Captains Eddie Stuart and Ross Dow.

Wolves beat the South Africans and defeated Celtic a fortnight later by another two-goal margin in front of 41,820. Racing Club of Buenos Aires went just the same way the following March, then the visits of First Vienna and Maccabi Tel Aviv in October, 1954 were marked by contrasting fortunes, with a draw and a ten-goal victory respectively. But all these were mere appetisers before the main feast.

Billy Wright and Bill Shorthouse (nearest camera) in respectful pose during the pre-match formalities on the occasion of Moscow Spartak's visit to take on League champions Wolves in November, 1954.

Moscow Spartak were tempted to Molineux in October and interest in their visit was sky-high. Molineux was buzzing with 55,184 packed inside as the floodgates opened after a goalless first half that contained near misses at both ends. Dennis Wilshaw opened the scoring in the 63rd minute following keeper Piraev's punch, then Johnny Hancocks (2) and Roy Swinbourne secured a 4-0 with goals in a storming finale - another show of the stamina and fitness of Cullis' players.

It was an occasion that transcended the sporting boundaries. Fifty members of Vono Cricket Club were holding their annual dinner at Dudley's Ward Arms Hotel on the same night but were determined to keep abreast of Molineux events. Their secretary had three televisions delivered to the function and insisted that the speeches were delayed until the match had finished.

The clash between east and west was greeted with nothing like the same level of enthusiasm on the other side of the Iron Curtain. Moscow Radio didn't mention it. All seven news bulletins broadcast in Russia that night ignored the game totally while Tass, the official Soviet news agency, did not carry a report. But a glowing tribute was heard on Moscow Radio's English-language service to the United States of America. "Our boys were treated to a fine display," it acknowledged.

Wolves in full cry as they attack the South Bank end in their memorable destruction of Spartak. This picture shows a Jimmy Mullen cross being dealt with.

eft: Dennis Wilshaw crashes in the first of Wolves' four goals against Moscow Spartak. The 4-0 win continued an pic series of Molineux matches and left the home players full of smiles afterwards.

Next up under the increasingly inspirational Molineux lights were a Honved side made up of many of the players who had humiliated England home and away in the run-up to the World Cup finals. Cullis, aware of his side's stamina, and the Magyars' mercurial talents, had his groundstaff boys, including Ron Atkinson, watering the pitch despite steady rain in the hours up to kick-off!

The ploy was designed to increase home advantage but seemed questionable as the visitors scorched across the sodden turf to take a match-winning grip in the first 15 minutes. Ferenc Puskas floated over a free-kick which was nodded past Bert Williams by Sandor Kocsis - described as the best header of the ball in the world - then Machos went through to make it two after Bozsik and Kocsis combined. Only Williams' heroics from Czibor kept Wolves in it, although Farago made a series of superb saves shortly before the interval from Swinbourne, Les Smith and Hancocks. Five minutes into the second half, the deficit was halved when Kovacs pushed Hancocks, who scored from the penalty. Seven Wolves corners and 25 minutes later came the equaliser as Bill Slater found

The Wolverhampton banquet trade was thriving as foreign visitors arrived at Molineux in the 1950s - and then left with their tails between their legs.

Wilshaw with a long pass and he crossed well for Swinbourne to head home.

Unbelievably, the same forward hit the winner only a minute later when Wilshaw's fine run put him clear. Even then, Williams had to save brilliantly to deny Czibor amid unbearable tension near the end. Wolves gallantly hung on to record what still stands as possibly the most famous of all the victories in their 128-year history; certainly one that will never be forgotten by the masses there to witness it.

It didn't need the pitch-watering exercise to signal how seriously the game was taken. The crowd themselves did that. The 54,998 turn-out on a misty, damp evening was 11,000 higher than

The most famous Molineux match of all - Roy Swinbourne challenges Honved's keeper Farago (left) and power home a header for the goal that made it 2-2 (right), with full-back Kovacs a spectator.

when Wolves clinched the title against Tottenham on a Saturday afternoon eight months earlier. So much for it being anything other than a highly competitive meeting of European giants.

Cullis later bemoaned the recording of such matches as friendlies, arguing vehemently: "Those fixtures were something out of the ordinary." And he found his keeper in full agreement: "No-one could call the Honved game a friendly," Williams said. "I classed it almost as another England v Hungary match. It was when you considered that they had so many of the players who had thrashed England, that you realised how satisfying the result was.

"But it certainly didn't make any of the players rich. We had six substitutes who had to share £2 because the Football Association would only allow 12 of us to have the win bonus of £2 each. And that was before tax. Apparently, if we had lost, we wouldn't have got anything."

The press described the victory as the rebirth of football in this country. Charles Buchan wrote: "Wolves, the League champions, struck a decisive blow for the British game with as wonderful a second-half rally as I have seen in 40 years." Roy Peskett said: "Wolves last night did what all the experts thought was impossible. They gave two goals' start to the side reckoned to be the best on the Continent and overhauled them."

The Times' correspondent wrote: "Wolverhampton did British football proud under the night sky. To recover two goals lost in the opening 14 minutes to such opposition, and then snatch the final victory, was a performance in skill, team spirit and stamina that needed no batteries and pylons of glittering arc lamps to illuminate it."

Millions heard the match live on the BBC - or at least most of it. With a minute left, listeners held their breath

> **RECOGNISING THE SADDLERS**
> "Which club did Wilshaw come from?" Billy Wright was asked by one of Honved's coaches. "What about Hancocks?" "And where did Williams play before Wolves." On being given the answer 'Walsall' each time, the coach raised his eyebrows and said: "Thank God we're not playing Walsall then."

Humble in victory as they lay down the welcome mat to their visitors - Wolves' players in the after-glow of another victory under the stirring Molineux floodlights in the 1954-55 season.

when Williams dived for the ball. Then they cursed their wirelesses as the commentary was suddenly taken off and replaced at the flick of a switch by The Show Band with 365 Kisses, the duty announcer saying calmly: "It is already half a minute past nine. I will give the final result later."

Immediately, complaints poured in. Such was the volume of furious calls that the switchboard in Birmingham was closed and protestors had to queue to get through to London to vent their anger. Half an hour later, The Show Band were taken off and an embarrassed voice uttered: "This is a very repentant Adrian Waller saying I realise I made a mistake fading out that great match. This is the kind of mistake we only make once."

BBC TV overran by five minutes to show the end of a match Cullis described as 'the most exciting I have ever seen.' And there was praise, too, from the beaten camp. Hungarian FA chairman Sandor Barcs sportingly said: "Wolves definitely deserved to win. They are a great team and I have never seen a greater centre-half than Billy Wright."

Williams added: "Billy was the player I was most pleased for. He'd had a bit of a run-around in the England-Hungary games, so to play against many of the same players and finish on the winning side was very satisfying. Stan was never very forthcoming with his praise. If you had a pat on the back, that was normally as good as it got. But, that night, he went out on the pitch, saying 'well done' to every one of us."

Swinbourne, making a habit of scoring heavily against foreign opposition, said: "That game was something else. Most historians say it was one of the greatest ever at Molineux, if not the greatest. With the lights and fluorescent shirts, it was pure theatre. Honved were brilliant but we were so strong in the last quarter. We were very fit and had skill as well. Throw in the team spirit and we were formidable."

One newspaper had already asked why the entire Wolves team couldn't be named to represent a languishing England, with the exception of reserve full-back Roy Pritchard in place of the South African Stuart. This, after all, was the match that had carried the club's name across the globe more than any other. But the heroic players had to wait until the following November to next pit their wits against foreign invaders.

Moscow Dynamo, like Spartak, had beaten Wolves on an unhappy summer tour of Russia six months earlier and had hammered Cardiff 10-1 on an earlier appearance within British shores. But they were defeated 2-1 in front of an enthralled 55,480 crowd that still stands as the highest ever for a friendly at the ground. Oops, there's that word 'friendly' again!

Hancocks and Jimmy Mullen teed up Slater to open the scoring in only the 14th minute and Jimmy Murray - on his first-team debut in place of the injured Swinbourne - sent Mullen through at a tight angle to find a second way past the legendary Russian international keeper Lev Yashin soon after half-time. Murray and Wilshaw went close and Fedeosov had a goal disallowed before Dynamo pulled one back through Ilyin, Wolves then holding on with relatively few alarms.

They had three wins out of three against mighty

Above: Under the glare of Molineux's famous lights, Dennis Wilshaw loses out to the Moscow Dynamo keeper, Piraev. Right: Another headache looms for the Russians' defence, on this occasion via Jimmy Murray. It was Murray's debut for Wolves, his League bow following three days later.

Continental opposition and their fans were lapping it up. These thrilling spectacles preceded the European Cup, although Cullis was among the first to spot the potential for such a competition, so Wolves' floodlit games were big news nationally. At a time when the club were also either winning or challenging for the League title, fans were in clover.

It was not until April, 1956 that Wolves first staged a First Division game under lights. Many teams were reluctant to play floodlit domestic matches and insisted where possible on kicking off earlier in the evening. But the series of Molineux glamour fixtures continued. Argentina's San Lorenzo were hammered early in that same year and Roumania CCA followed suit before Red Banner restored some Hungarian pride by emerging from the gold and black fortress with a draw.

In the spring of 1957 came Borussia Dortmund and Valencia - both of whom were beaten - then it was time to unfurl the welcome mat in the October for arguably the best club in the world. The European Cup had by now been launched and Real Madrid won it in the first two years, 1956 and 1957, beating Manchester United in the semi-final on one occasion. Now they were booked in for an outing under Molineux's improved lights.

The Spaniards did not come to England cheap and the West Midlands public were asked to dig a little deeper for the privilege of watching them. But, despite the absence of Wright because of international duty, Wolves still brought their illustrious visitors down a notch or two in front of another 55,000-plus crowd after Marsal had opened the scoring with a bullet header.

Soon after half-time, Broadbent's lob deflected in off Marquitos to bring the equaliser after Murray nodded on Malcolm Finlayson's long kick, then Murray turned finisher supreme to make it 2-1 with a fine header from Norman Deeley's corner on the hour. Mighty Real bounced back with Marsal levelling, only for Wilshaw to fire the winner ten minutes from time from Mullen's centre.

The shockwaves rumbled all the way back to Madrid. The European champions, the kings of the Continent, weren't supposed to lose, so they promptly invited Wolves to Spain for a return two months later on December 11, 1957. It was set up as a revenge mission; for the matador to have his moment in front of his adoring public. Only Cullis' men refused to roll over and die.

This time, it finished 2-2, only an offside-looking goal by substitute Mateo saving Real's five-year unbeaten home record in the first winter floodlit game they had staged. Bobby Mason's header to Mullen's cross stunned the rain-lashed 60,000 crowd and, although Alfredo Di Stefano made it 2-1, Mullen's cross was sliced in by a defender for a deserved equaliser nine minutes from time.

The combined efforts of Gerry Harris and keeper Malcolm Finlayson fail to stop Marsal scoring for Real Madrid at Molineux. But Wolves again hit back to win famously.

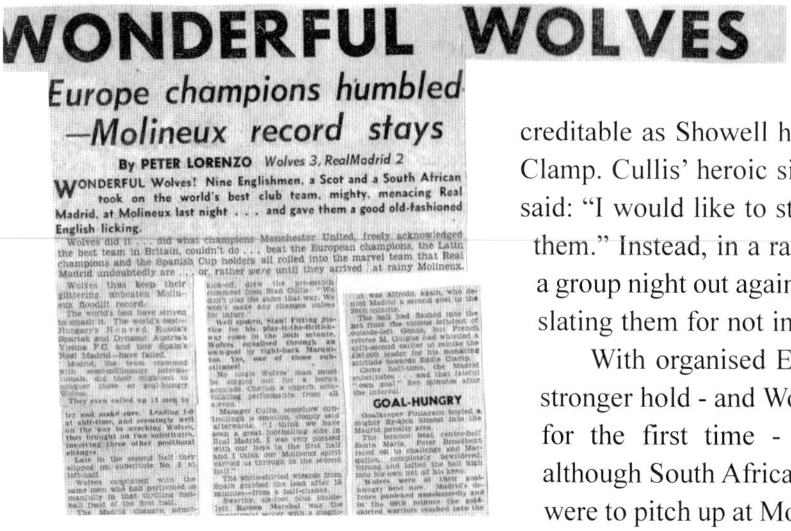

WONDERFUL WOLVES

Europe champions humbled —Molineux record stays

By PETER LORENZO Wolves 3, RealMadrid 2

WONDERFUL Wolves! Nine Englishmen, a Scot and a South African took on the world's best club team, mighty, menacing Real Madrid, at Molineux last night . . . and gave them a good old-fashioned English licking.

Wolves did it . . . did what champions Manchester United, freely acknowledged the best team in Britain, couldn't do . . . beat the European champions, the Latin champions and the Spanish Cup holders all rolled into the marvel team that Real Madrid undoubtedly are . . . or, rather *were* until they arrived at rainy Molineux.

Wolves thus keep their glittering, unbeaten Molineux floodlit record.

The world's best have striven to smash it. The world's best—Hungary's Honved, Russia's Spartak and Dynamo, Austria's Vienna F.C. and now Spain's Real Madrid—have failed.

Madrid, the team crammed with semi-millionaire internationals, did their mightiest to conquer these so goal-hungry Wolves.

They even called up 14 men to try and make sure. Leading 1-0 at half-time, and seemingly well on the way to wrecking Wolves, they brought on two substitutes, involving three other positional changes.

Late in the second half they slipped on substitute No. 3 at left-half.

Wolves continued with the same men who had performed so manfully in that thrilling football feast of the first half.

The Madrid changes, admitted after the kick-off, drew the pre-match comment from Stan Cullis: "We don't play the game that way. We won't make any changes unless for injury."

Well spoken, Stan! Fitting justice for his play-it-the-British-way come in the 50th minute. Wolves equalised through an own-goal by right-back Marquitos. Yes, one of those substitutes!

No single Wolves' man must be singled out for a hero's accolade. Cherish a superb, scintillating performance from all eleven.

Manager Cullis, somehow controlling his emotion, simply said afterwards: "I think we have seen a great footballing side in Real Madrid. I was very pleased with our boys in the first half and I think our Molineux spirit carried us through in the second half."

The white-shirted wizards from Spain grabbed the lead after 15 minutes—from a half-chance.

Swarthy, six-foot plus inside-left Ramon Marshal was the ...

It was Alfredo, again, who denied Madrid a second goal in the 38th minute.

The ball had flashed into the net from the vicious left-foot of outside-left Gento, but French referee M. Guigue had whistled a split-second earlier to rebuke the £90,000 leader for his menacing attitude towards Eddie Clamp.

Came half-time, the Madrid substitutes . . . and that fateful "own goal" five minutes after the interval.

GOAL-HUNGRY

Goalkeeper Finlayson booted a mighty fly-kick almost into the Madrid penalty area.

The bounce beat centre-half Santa Maria. Peter Broadbent raced on to challenge and Marquitos, completely bewildered, turned and lofted the ball high into his own net off his knee.

Wolves were at their goal-hungry best now. Madrid's defence panicked unashamedly and in the 68th minute the gold-shirted warriors crashed into the

It was described as Wolves' finest hour on a foreign field, all the more creditable as Showell had replaced the injured Eddie Clamp. Cullis' heroic side were magnificent and he said: "I would like to strike a medal for every one of them." Instead, in a rare show of defiance, they had a group night out against orders and had the manager slating them for not inviting him along, too!

With organised European competition taking a stronger hold - and Wolves soon becoming involved for the first time - the 'friendlies' petered out, although South Africa, Tbilisi Dynamo and Honved were to pitch up at Molineux up to December, 1962. It was the end of a chapter; a chapter that had made Wolverhampton Wanderers world-renowned pioneers of prestige floodlit fixtures.

Molineux's Floodlit Specials

September 30, 1953: ***Wolves 3 South Africa 1*** (Mullen, Broadbent, Swinbourne)
October 14, 1953: ***Wolves 2 Celtic 0*** (Wilshaw 2)
March 10, 1954: ***Wolves 3 Buenos Aires 1*** (Taylor, Deeley, Mullen)
October 13, 1954: ***Wolves 0 First Vienna 0***
October 28, 1954: ***Wolves 10 Maccabi 0*** (Swinbourne 3, Hancocks 2, Broadbent 2, Flowers, McDonald, Wilshaw)
November 16, 1954: ***Wolves 4 Moscow Spartak 0*** (Hancocks 2, Swinbourne, Wilshaw)
December 13, 1954: ***Wolves 3 Honved 2*** (Hancocks pen, Swinbourne 2)
November 9, 1955: ***Wolves 2 Moscow Dynamo 1*** (Slater, Mullen)
January 28, 1956: ***Wolves 5 San Lorenzo 1*** (Broadbent 3, Hancocks, Wilshaw)
October 29, 1956: ***Wolves 5 Roumania CCA 0*** (Murray 2, Hooper pen, Broadbent, Booth)
December 11, 1956: ***Wolves 1 Red Banner 1*** (Neil)
March 27, 1957: ***Wolves 4 Borussia Dortmund 3*** (Broadbent, Murray, Wilshaw, Hooper)
April 10, 1957: ***Wolves 3 Valencia 0*** (Thomson 2, Clamp)
October 17, 1957: ***Wolves 3 Real Madrid 2*** (Broadbent, Murray, Wilshaw)
September 29, 1958: ***Wolves 1 South Africa X1 0*** (Horne)
November 10, 1960: ***Wolves 5 Dynamo Tbilisi 5*** (Farmer 2, Murray, Mason, Durandt)
December 3, 1962: ***Wolves 1 Honved 1*** (Hinton)

1955-56

Challenging Again

Roy Swinbourne has more reason than most to remember Wolves' 1955-56 campaign - and he saw barely a third of it. It started with him in electrifying form and with a first England call looking a certainty. It ended with his football career in ruins; another of the game's hard-luck stories.

The tall Yorkshireman scored in an opening-day draw at Albion, then cut loose in a devastating burst of form. On three successive Saturdays from late August, he hit hat-tricks - against Manchester City, Cardiff and Huddersfield, turning the first of them against regular whipping boys City into a four-goal haul. Wolves won that game 7-2 but their crushing margin of victory was to be dwarfed by a 9-1 landslide at Cardiff the other side of a more routine victory over Portsmouth.

Wolves' spectacular success at Ninian Park was the biggest post-war victory by an English club in a top-flight away fixture, equalling an all-time record that had stood since 1908. It contained a second treble, this time from Johnny Hancocks but was followed by some not totally unexpected

Albion goalkeeper Jim Sanders' safe handling denies Dennis Wilshaw and Bill Slater in a Hawthorns stalemate on the first day of 1955-56.

Wolves' goal-hungry forwards await the arrival of a free-kick in the big home win over Huddersfield.

criticism from the man who had overseen it all. "Nine floppin' goals and you could only flippin' score one!" said manager Stan Cullis to Jimmy Mullen.

Swinbourne was having no such problems in the marksman department and kindly put a good word in for the left-winger in a subsequent TV interview in which he complimented him for having a hand in eight of the side's nine goals. It was a tribute that had the grateful Geordie smiling: "Thanks for the thought Roy. I'll point that out to Stan!"

Bill Slater was another to find praise in very short supply. "I expected a pat on the back after a result like that," he said. "Instead, I was given a half-hour lecture on why Cardiff had been allowed to score near the end. And by then we were nine up! Stan was a very demanding manager but I knew that from the day I signed. He said to me then: 'I have to pay you a £10 signing-on fee, not that I think you're worth it.'"

After the carnage of Cardiff, Swinbourne scored three as Huddersfield escaped from Molineux on the end of a 4-0 scoreline that looked respectable by comparison. The opening six matches had brought four wins and 25 goals and Swinbourne was at it again with braces at home to Chelsea and away to Manchester United, the club who were destined to succeed the Londoners as title winners.

In all, he had scored an astonishing 17 times in 11 games and the world seemed to be his oyster. Having won a B cap against Germany at Hillsborough the previous spring and marked the occasion with a goal, he appeared well set for promotion to the senior team. In fact, he was unofficially told that he was to be named for the full international in Denmark at the beginning of October. But big disappointment was in store.

"I think it was our director, Mr Oakley, who told me I would be selected," he recalls. "It seemed a certainty I was in because I was scoring plenty of goals but I put the radio on and heard that Nat

Lofthouse had been chosen instead. The game in Copenhagen was to be played on a Sunday and the FA had decided that only one player from each club would be named. With Billy as skipper, that was that."

At around the same juncture, Swinbourne was in the showers following training one day when Cullis enquired about his age. On being told the centre-forward was 26, he said: "I'll have to be looking for a replacement for you before much longer then." The comment was typical of the way the manager kept players' feet on terra firma but it also proved to be a sad prophecy. Swinbourne suffered a serious knee injury only a few days later and was clutching a one-way ticket towards retirement.

His problems started in a 5-1 roasting at Luton on Bonfire Night afternoon - a game in which Bobby Mason lined up at inside-right for his debut. "I chased a ball to the byeline and pulled a muscle in the back of my thigh," Swinbourne

Roy Swinbourne has two young admirers as company during his otherwise lonely, long battle for fitness. Below left: Eddie Stuart, who was a potential inspiration to him after his own recovery.

said. "A lot of reports said I was sidestepping the photographers but it was actually some youngsters I was struggling to avoid because it was a full house and they were sitting by the edge of the pitch.

"I didn't play for a month and, when I did, it was at Preston, where things just became worse. I turned when I was challenged by Tommy Docherty and my knee twisted under me quite badly. I'm sure it was caused by my muscle not having strengthened again properly following the earlier injury.

We had a doctor with us at Preston and he said he said he thought it would be all right. But, three operations later, it was clear to me that it wasn't going to improve sufficiently.

"I'd suffered both cartilage and cruciate damage which wouldn't be career-threatening these days. But it was too bad for the medical people to repair at that time. I was 26 when I suffered the injury and 27 when I finally had to call it a day. I kept getting fluid on my knee whenever I exerted myself in training or in matches in the junior teams and, although I had

Wolves' early exit from the 1955-56 FA Cup left them free to squeeze in another game against foreign opposition in mid-winter, this one against San Lorenzo from Argentina kicking off in the relative light of a murky January afternoon. A sometimes bad-tempered 5-1 home victory contained a hat-trick from Peter Broadbent - and three Wolves penalties. Johnny Hancocks took all three and missed two.

encouragement from Stan and the specialist in Waterloo Road, Mr Freeman, I knew that was it."

Swinbourne's total of seven hat-tricks was a post-war record and, over 230 competitive games, he was only one goal short of averaging exactly one for every two matches - a terrific record. As he strove manfully against the odds and tried various comebacks in the reserves, he had Eddie Stuart as inspiration. The defender recovered from a life-threatening illness to re-establish himself late in 1953-54 and then play 37 and 38 games respectively in the following two seasons.

But the Swinbourne tale did not end anything like as happily and the loss to Wolves was only exceeded by the personal pain and anguish of a man who had seen his career snatched away before it reached its peak. "I don't think I was much fun to live with for a while," he now says.

In his place, Jimmy Murray made a good start with 11 goals in 25 games after promotion from the reserves but Wolves missed the experienced man. They lost seven League games in 12, although there was a highlight at home to Charlton in November when Bill Shorthouse, by now established at left-back after Billy Wright's switch to centre-half, scored the first and last goal of his 376-game Wanderers career.

He couldn't prevent an extraordinary turnaround in fortunes on New Year's Eve, though. Wolves had gone a full year without a home defeat and at one stage reeled off 12 successive

A familiar 1950s celebrations scene in the home dressing room at Molineux. From left, Bert Williams, Dennis Wilshaw, Eddie Stuart, Leslie Smith, Bill Shorthouse, Johnny Hancocks and Billy Wright are the happy men here but Wolves didn't have as much to savour in 1955-56 as in many other seasons.

Molineux victories before finally being beaten in front of their own fans. The fact that it was by the Cardiff side slammed 9-1 by them at Ninian Park four months earlier merely added to the disbelief.

When Albion avenged an earlier League defeat at the ground by crossing the Black Country to triumph in an FA Cup third-round tie, Wolves had only second place to aim for. The Manchester United side who were to complete a First Division double over them were so far ahead in the table that runners-up spot was the extent of everyone else's ambitions.

Although Wolves completed a double over champions Chelsea with a terrific win at Stamford Bridge, they lost home and away to Blackpool, and had a poor Easter week as 0-0 draws against Aston Villa in successive days were followed by a defeat at Everton.

It was Blackpool who duly followed United home, Matt Busby's men securing the title with two games remaining as their winning margin of 11 points set an English record. Wolves had the consolation of finishing strongly and were ultimately beaten to second place only on goal average, a final-day draw at relegated Sheffield United costing them runners-up spot.

They signed off with four wins and a draw - including two points against Tottenham on the night floodlights were used at Molineux for a League match for the first time - as Dennis Wilshaw finally found some scoring form at the end of a less prolific club campaign. He had netted twice for England against Northern Ireland at Wembley and once against Finland in Helsinki but was more restrained at club level.

As he notched three times in four League games, there was also a show of composure from

Peter Broadbent is denied by Sunderland's John Bollands in Wolves' final home game of 1955-56 - a match they still won 3-1.

Slater, who scored four penalties in April before Colin Booth rattled in a memorable last-day hat-trick in an entertaining draw at Bramall Lane - still one of Wolves' happiest and most fruitful hunting grounds.

Hancocks nevertheless led the club goal charts for the second year running, having also finished joint top scorer with Jesse Pye back in 1947-48. It's strange to reflect after a season's haul of 18 that took his Molineux career total to 166 from 378 appearances, that he didn't play another competitive Wolves first-team game. His knack as a quality and often fearsome finisher by no means deserted him but his 24 goals the following season all came in the reserves before he drifted into non-League. And that 1956-57 campaign was to represent the calm before Wolverhampton Wanderers took English football by storm.

AN UNHAPPY LANDING

Bill Slater missed Wolves' draw at Sheffield United in May, 1955 - but not through injury, loss of form or England duty. He was absent because efforts to fly him to the match backfired when the plane landed at the wrong airfield!

"The Everall brothers, who ran the coach company in the town, were on the board of directors at the time and had a two-seater that was piloted by one of the sons," Slater recalled. "We couldn't find the airfield we were meant to land at and where, apparently, there was someone from the club waving a towel to try to attract our attention.

"We landed by mistake at an RAF airfield near to Worksop, which meant I had to hitch-hike the rest of the way to Sheffield. But I arrived there too late for the match and don't think Stan Cullis was too pleased."

WATH WANDERERS - A RICH SEAM OF TALENT

There's not much trace now of one of English football's most fertile breeding grounds. But the names of Mark Crook and Wath Wanderers should be etched forever in Wolves fans' memories.

Ron Flowers, Roy Swinbourne, John Short, Joe Bonson, Geoff Sidebottom, Barry Stobart, Ken Knighton, Peter Knowles, Gerry Taylor, Bob Hatton and Steve Daley were all products of the famous nursery Crook developed in the Stan Cullis era.

The diminutive winger impressed Cullis sufficiently during his own unspectacular Molineux playing career as to be entrusted with unearthing gems from the mining areas of south Yorkshire. At a colliery ground in Wath-upon-Dearne deep in Arthur Scargill country - seven miles west of the M1 near Doncaster - he took over the facilities of Brampton Welfare FC to form Wath Wanderers.

"He was set up by Stan and would recommend his best lads to Wolves," said Flowers, who headed for Molineux around the same time as another Wath boy, Dick Neal. "I remember Stan going to Wath to watch games.

"They played in a men's league but the Wolves Juniors side played Leeds, Newcastle, Middlesbrough, Sunderland, Barnsley, the Sheffield teams and Hull in the Northern Intermediate League. I was with them for a year and remember playing Newcastle at St James' Park one Saturday morning and then being taken to watch Wolves play at Sunderland in the afternoon. That was a thrill as I'd never watched a first-team match. I was very keen to see Roy Swinbourne and tried to emulate him."

1956-57

On The Launch Pad

Top sides, it is said, are made up of artists and artisans; players with the gift of turning the key at one end and those capable of bolting the door at the other. Wolves were blessed with both types. Their crowd-pleasing qualities came to be underlined in trophies and records but they were not short of a bit of brawn either - a commodity that surfaced even on the training ground.

Players used to try to wangle a place in Bill Shorthouse's side in practice games as the defender didn't take those contests much easier than he treated match-days. The intense competition for places ensured the annual colours v whites games were very keen, too, and Eddie Stuart recalls: "I faced Jimmy Mullen a couple of times and remember him saying: 'Don't you bloody kick me.' He used to cross the ball without taking it round me first!"

So adept was Stuart at fending for himself, like Shorthouse, Eddie Clamp and Bill Slater, that after one game at Liverpool, Billy Liddell asked Billy Wright: "Blimey, what do they feed him on? Raw meat?" Perhaps the desire to succeed was fired by the *need* to succeed, because even the top players couldn't afford to collect houses and cars like they do today.

"I lived in a house at Penn that I rented off the club," said keeper Malcolm Finlayson. "If you weren't retained, you were not only out of the club and out of a job but also out of a home - often with a young family. The wages in football were so much lower then and players had to be prepared to travel the country to find a club, so there was a lot of pressure on you to make sure you were on that retained list."

Wolves were certainly hungry as they went into 1956-57, having just finished first, second and third in the previous three seasons. Johnny Hancocks' place went immediately to Harry Hooper, a

Bill Shorthouse (in background) - managing a smile and always setting the right example.

81

Bill Shorthouse and no 2 Eddie Stuart look on as Bert Williams punches clear in Wolves' defeat at Luton in their first away game. The keeper was by now under pressure from Malcolm Finlayson.

former Durham County Youth team-mate of Bobby Robson's, whose £25,000 switch from West Ham made him England's costliest winger as well as a club record signing. He marked his Wolves debut by scoring in the opening-day trouncing of Manchester City but was eclipsed by four-goal Jimmy Murray.

After two away defeats, Murray then netted a brace in a sensational home clash with Luton. Wolves were two down in ten minutes, 5-3 up at half-time and won 5-4. Gordon Turner achieved the rarity of scoring a hat-trick for a losing side - and the recently signed Finlayson said: "That was the best match I've ever seen. There were nine goals and both Bert Williams and the Luton keeper, Bernard Streten, had great games."

Dumbarton-born Finlayson had first caught the eye of Molineux scout George Noakes in a similar game at Walsall for Millwall in 1948. "I went to hospital for stitches to my face when we were 1-0 up," he said. "When I returned, we were 3-1 down and I couldn't get back into the ground until the director with me jumped over a wall. We pulled back to win 6-5, though, with Walsall hitting the bar in the last few moments!"

Finlayson, who also attracted strong interest from Charlton, left Millwall because they didn't want him pursuing a sales career on his afternoons off - an arrangement Stan Cullis was happy with. Williams was part-time anyway, juggling training on two or three mornings a week with running a sports outfitters in Bath Street, Bilston and coaching kids at night in a sports centre he had opened.

Cullis paid £4,000 for Finlayson and gave him a 12-game run in the autumn, soon after Slater had scored in three consecutive matches from right-half. With Williams sidelined by a split bone in his finger, the Scot's debut was a 2-1 home defeat against a John Charles-inspired Leeds before his

first away match came a week later at Bolton, where he kept his first Wolves clean sheet in a comprehensive win.

It was also the day he learned of the extraordinary lengths Cullis went to in the search for perfection.

Peter Broadbent for once fails to cash in on this clear scoring chance during Sunderland's midweek visit to Molineux early in the 1956-57 season.

"We were three up at half-time and I was whistling on my way in at half-time because I was enjoying it so much," he says. "But by the time I reached the corridor leading to the dressing room, I could hear Stan berating two players as we weren't six up! Even when we were playing so well, he wanted more."

A derby-day draw at West Brom followed by a 6-0 hiding of fading Portsmouth and an astonishing 3-3 draw at Chelsea from three down with only 15 minutes left to play were other notable early markings on the Finlayson graph as the autumn continued to be packed with highlights, even if Wolves were also struggling for consistency.

Hooper netted in five games

Noel Dwyer, one of Wolves' reserve keepers, prepares to dive at the feet of Roy Swinbourne during a training work-out at Patshull.

in a row before Colin Booth, a Manchester-born inside-forward who had scored seven times the season before, including the last of the club's five 1955-56 hat-tricks, cut loose with four goals in the 5-2 rout of Arsenal.

The spotlight was back on Hooper via a hat-trick in another astonishing comeback, Wolves this time rallying from 3-0 down to beat Preston with three goals in the last 15 minutes on the day Clamp played his first game of the season and Bobby Mason equalised in only his second full match.

There was a feeling of evolution about Cullis' team. Although Billy Wright, Ron Flowers, Peter Broadbent and Mullen were still regulars, Molineux fans had seen the last of another stalwart, Shorthouse. Time had caught up with him at 34, wear-and-tear problems with his ankle helping see to it that he didn't reappear in the competitive arena after the 3-0 home win over Birmingham.

Signed as an amateur way back in 1941, he played in every round of the 1949 FA Cup triumph, all but two matches in the winning of the 1953-54 League Championship and stood in regularly as captain when Wright was with England. Most remarkably, he had never been dropped. And to think it might all have ended before it had really begun.....

Shorthouse, trained at Worcester Barracks, was a member of the South Staffs Regiment and saw very active service in the war, disembarking from one of the first boats during the Normandy landings. "Our job was to lay explosives on the beach and gain control of a bridge," he added. "As you can imagine, it was very frightening. The place was mined and cast-iron crosses had been erected to stop the tanks.

"There was a lot of firing and a bullet went through my backside and hit my arm. Funnily enough, it didn't hurt a lot but I lost plenty of blood and couldn't hold a gun, so I had to wait six or seven hours for a boat to take me back to England. I came back to hospital in Epping and didn't see active service after that. I was sent to Halifax and Chester for the rest of my time in the Army.

"I know there were an awful lot of casualties in operations like that and many brave men lost their lives. But we were lucky not to have many in our regiment. I still have the scar on my left arm and have frequently counted my blessings. I suppose if I had been struck in the leg, it could easily have caused an injury serious enough to have scuppered my football career."

The one regret he came to have, after a period during which so many families were ripped apart, was purely a football one; namely, that his excellent club career failed to open any doors to the international stage. Even when he was called up by the Football League for a game against the Irish League, he was ultimately left out.

As Gerry Harris stepped in at left-back for Shorthouse, having made his debut in the extraordinary Luton game, hostilities elsewhere in the world dictated that Wolves had had to do without Norman Deeley. Although long since demobbed from Army duties that had taken him to Northern Ireland, the 23-year-old was called back as a result of the 1956 Suez Crisis.

"It was a shock because my football career was getting off the ground and we were expecting

our first child," he said. "But the country had to come first. Three oil ships had been sunk in Egypt and we were sent over there to unload ammunition, tanks and supplies, 12 hours on, 12 hours off. We lived in a school for six months and there was no time for football after the day's work. I had to forget about the game for a long, long while."

Deeley would return in the latter stages of a campaign that continued to ebb and flow excitingly. Blackpool were sent home empty-handed by a hat-trick from Dennis Wilshaw on a misty pre-Christmas afternoon but the forward was generally on the fringes of the side - a situation that probably kept him out of England's 5-2 World Cup qualifier victory over Denmark at Molineux in early December.

The 12th cap Wilshaw won in the autumn proved to be his last while Broadbent was still unrecognised at senior level despite scoring six times in four matches straight after a Christmas Day defeat at relegation-bound Charlton. Wolves' unpredictability and huge goal-scoring potential were making them great entertainers but they remained frustratingly short of the title-winning standard.

Bill Slater and Billy Wright in the thick of things at Chelsea, who followed their title triumph of 1955 by finishing 16th and then 13th in the next two years.

The concession of three first-half goals at Everton contributed to an eighth defeat in 12 away games and, despite a follow-up win at Sunderland secured when Joe Bonson marked his League debut by making all three goals, manager Cullis was sufficiently discomforted by what he was seeing as to miss the home victory over Tottenham in favour of going player-watching in Scotland.

In the FA Cup, Wolves beat Second Division Swansea 5-3, Bonson scoring two on his home debut, only to then fall to Bournemouth from Division Three South. It may not quite have ranked with England v USA in 1950 but it was still one of the biggest-ever shocks in the competition. Williams, Wright and Mullen played both in Belo Horizonte and in the Molineux embarrassment, which was sealed by a goal from ex-Albion winger Reg Cutler on a day the goal post at the South Bank end snapped following a collision.

The only whiff of FA Cup success Molineux was to experience that season was when Wolves staged the FA Cup semi-final between Albion and Aston Villa, and Slater said: "I don't remember much about the Bournemouth game other than the post incident and the fact I got an injury which made me a passenger for a while. But that defeat was my lowest ebb at the club."

Wolves had troubles of a different kind when their train broke down en route for the League match at Leeds, causing them to change on the coach to Elland Road and for kick-off to be delayed by seven minutes. Maybe the unhelpful preparation contributed to the goalless draw but, if away results were rocky, Wolves were devastating in home League games.

When they beat Bolton 3-2, Hooper scored twice and was denied a hat-trick only when his penalty was saved by Nat Lofthouse - in goal for 25 minutes because of an injury to Eddie Hopkinson. Then Charlton were hit for seven, Bonson kicking off a run of three goals in successive games, before Chelsea, Newcastle, Albion and Villa were also sent home with their tails between their legs. Wolves beat Albion at Molineux for the fourth year running but one scalp they couldn't

Bert Williams in Wolves action at Manchester City in his hey-day..... now he was near to retirement as 1956-57 wore on.

take was that of Manchester United. The 1956 champions drew at the ground in mid-March in front of 53,000 and again marched clear to take the crown by eight points, Cullis' men's failure to win any of their final eight away matches ensuring they could finish no better than sixth in the search for talent money.

The last of those defeats on the road - just down the road, in fact - marked the end of Bert Williams' quite magnificent career. In a 4-0 Easter Monday loss at Villa, he was injured when hitting the post as he dived. "The return against Villa was the next day and I was still sore, so I missed that one," he said. "It was a sad way to finish but that was it. I was generally very fortunate."

Wolves won 3-0 just 24 hours later - results often contrasted vividly when clubs met twice in successive days - and Williams melted away into the business world after 420 League and Cup games for the club, numerous prestige matches against Continental sides, and 24 England caps. There were no newspaper pull-outs, no laps of honour, just a quiet exit.

"I only played in the reserves a couple of times and didn't want to go back to Molineux a few days later for a last game in the reserves, as the secretary Jack Howley suggested," he added. "Even if I had played a farewell game and said cheerio to the fans, though, there wouldn't have been any fuss. There wasn't the same fanfare then."

Williams, whose appearance tally was a record for a Wolves keeper, left in the same summer as Hancocks, his colleague at Walsall and Molineux for 19 years. "I obviously regret losing six years of my football life to the war but I had a tremendous career," he added. "Today's players can have their £50,000 a week. I've got loads of friends round the world, so I'm happy."

Finlayson, an ex-RAF driving instructor who had played at Molineux in a 1953 match against the Army that also featured Flowers and Broadbent, took over in the revenge win over Villa, who were to beat Manchester United in the FA Cup final 11 days later. It was Wolves' last match of the season and was soon followed by the formal retirement of Shorthouse, another of the club's true stalwarts.

Fortunately, the defender had other strings to his bow and says: "After I'd decided I couldn't play any longer, Joe Gardiner told me Stan wanted to see me. The first thing he said was that he wanted to offer me a coaching job. It softened the blow a lot and helped me out when I needed it. Obviously, I took it and spent many years coaching at Wolves before working with England youths, Villa and Birmingham."

The change of roles brought some wry smiles in the dressing room he was leaving behind. That formidable training-game opponent for many years among the bricks, stones and glass on the Molineux car park, would clearly be no pushover in his new role. "We knew he would be a hard task-master as a coach as well but Stan wouldn't have wanted anything else," said one of his team-mates.

Hooper's fine debut season left him top scorer

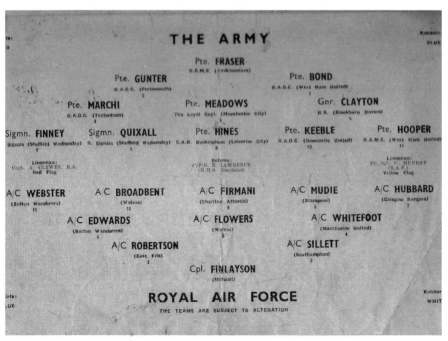

The 1953 Army v RAF clash at Molineux - a wealth of talent on view.

ITINERARY

Wolverhampton Wanderers Football Club

APRIL, 1957

SAT. 27th	
1.00 p.m.	Depart LONDON by air.
SUN. 28th	
1.35 p.m.	Arrive JOHANNESBURG (Jan Smuts Airport). Proceed by motor coach to and stay at the Victoria Hotel.

MAY, 1957

SAT. 4th	*MATCH AGAINST SOUTHERN TRANSVAAL.*
WED. 8th	Proceed by motor coach to PRETORIA.
	MATCH AGAINST COMBINED NORTHERN AND EASTERN TRANSVAAL.
	Return to hotel after the match.
THURS. 9th	
6.00 a.m.	Proceed by motor coach to Jan Smuts Airport.
7.45 a.m.	Depart JOHANNESBURG by S.A. Airways Flight S.A.317.
9.30 a.m.	Arrive DURBAN (Louis Botha Airport). Proceed by motor coach to and stay at the Park View Hotel.
SAT. 11th	*MATCH AGAINST NATAL.*

MON. 13th	
8.45 a.m.	Proceed by motor coach to Louis Botha Airport.
10.00 a.m.	Depart DURBAN by S.A. Airways Flight S.A.319.
3.30 p.m.	Arrive CAPE TOWN (D. F. Malan Airport). Proceed by motor coach to and stay at the International Hotel.
WED. 15th	*MATCH AGAINST WESTERN PROVINCE.*
THURS. 16th	
3.45 p.m.	Proceed by motor coach to D. F. Malan Airport.
5.00 p.m.	Depart CAPE TOWN by S.A. Airways Flight S.A.302.
8.45 p.m.	Arrive JOHANNESBURG (Jan Smuts Airport). Proceed by motor coach to and stay at the Victoria Hotel.
SAT. 18th	*MATCH AGAINST A SOUTH AFRICAN XI.*
WED. 22nd	
10.15 a.m.	Proceed by motor coach to Jan Smuts Airport.
11.45 a.m.	Depart JOHANNESBURG by S.A. Airways Flight S.A.250.
1.50 p.m.	Arrive BULAWAYO (Kumalo Airport). Proceed by Central African Airways transport to and stay at the Cecil Hotel.
FRI. 24th	*MATCH AGAINST SOUTHERN RHODESIA.*
SAT. 25th	
5.45 a.m.	Proceed by Central African Airways transport to Kumalo Airport.
6.30 a.m.	Depart BULAWAYO by Central African Airways Flight C.E.640.
8.00 a.m.	Arrive SALISBURY.
9.15 a.m.	Depart SALISBURY by Central African Airways Flight C.E.900.
10.50 a.m.	Arrive NDOLA. Proceed by private transport to KITWE and stay at the Nkana Hotel.
SUN. 26th	*MATCH AGAINST NORTHERN RHODESIA.*
WED. 29th	
a.m.	Proceed by private transport to Ndola Airport.
10.35 a.m.	Depart NDOLA by Central African Airways Flight C.E.804.
3.20 p.m.	Arrive NAIROBI.
8.15 p.m.	Depart NAIROBI by S.A. Airways Flight S.A.214.
THURS. 30th	
11.10 a.m.	Arrive LONDON.

with 19, followed by Broadbent (18) and the blossoming Murray (17). Wolves' tally of home League goals was a fabulous 70, only their shortcomings on away grounds, where they managed just 24, keeping them so far adrift of top three Manchester United, Tottenham and Preston.

United relied heavily on youth and it's easy to believe that Matt Busby was influenced by events at Molineux. It is well documented that the Old Trafford legend spent many hours during the war chewing the fat with Cullis, who would no doubt have regaled him with tales of how the 'Buckley Babes' had evolved at Wolves in the 1930s. And, just as Cullis was short-changed when the praise and honours were distributed among contemporaries such as Bill Shankly, Jock Stein, Bill Nicholson and, yes, Busby, so Major Frank Buckley's vision in identifying home-grown talent as the way forward has been allowed to fade too easily from the public perception.

Predictably, goals flowed at one end but not the other when Cullis' Wolves departed early in the close season on their second visit in seven summers to South Africa. A seven-game itinerary spanning nearly a month was drawn up, although there was considerable disappointment among the locals that the 33-year-old Wright had to stay behind to play three matches for England - two against the Republic of Ireland and one against Denmark.

Stuart took over as skipper, his film-star looks leading to him being described in his country's press as 'a bronzed Adonis.' Not that his wages matched the movie legends. He'd even had a taste of the more mundane life at Sankey's factory in Bilston, where he was no stranger to having his backside pinched by admiring females whose wages could reach £25 a week on piece-rate - about twice as high as his football money!

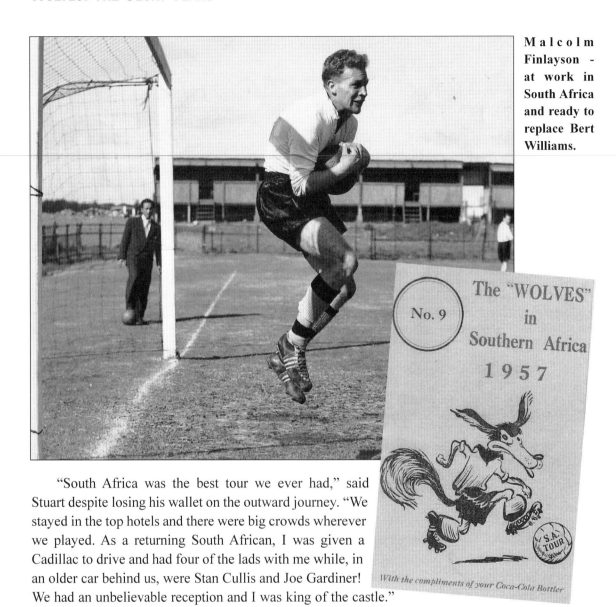

Malcolm Finlayson - at work in South Africa and ready to replace Bert Williams.

The "WOLVES" in Southern Africa 1957

No. 9

S.A. TOUR

With the compliments of your Coca-Cola Bottler

"South Africa was the best tour we ever had," said Stuart despite losing his wallet on the outward journey. "We stayed in the top hotels and there were big crowds wherever we played. As a returning South African, I was given a Cadillac to drive and had four of the lads with me while, in an older car behind us, were Stan Cullis and Joe Gardiner! We had an unbelievable reception and I was king of the castle."

So popular did Wolves prove as they reeled off a succession of victories on their exhausting travels that they were asked to find a spare slot in their schedule. They were invited to play an extra fixture in mid-tour under the new lights at Johannesburg's Rand Stadium. They duly obliged and again gave terrific value for money by winning handsomely against a President's X1 for whom a

SUNDAY TIMES, JOHANNESBURG, TRANSVAAL, MAY 5. 1957.

HAIL THE GREATEST FOOTBALL MACHINE TO VISIT SOUTH AFRICA IN POST-WAR YE

Murray's 5 for Wolves—Team of Dyn

S. TRANSVAAL . . 2, WOLVES . . 5

CALL them a team of mechanical footballers . . . call them human thoroughbreds . . . or even eleven dynamos . . . but whatever you may call them this Wolverhampton Wanderers side are the slickest, smartest and most penetrating soccer machine to visit South Africa since the war.

A Rand Stadium crowd of 39,000 saw them score five — all to centre-forward Jim Murray — and give a wonderful exhibition of ball play at a tremendous speed on a greasy ground in the opening

The South African press had no doubt - Wolves were the best side they had seen.

talented young man called Cliff Durandt impressed with two goals in his side's 7-3 defeat.

Wright, having played in crushing England wins over the Republic of Ireland and Denmark and a draw away to the Irish, joined his club colleagues for their final two matches - in the country known these days as Zimbabwe. Wolves were greeted on touchdown in Bulawayo by a small group of immigrants from Wolverhampton 'sporting gold and black favours' - and signed off by registering double-figure scores against both Southern Rhodesia and Northern Rhodesia.

Despite a torturous 54-hour return journey, caused by heavy flooding at Nairobi Airport and a diversion via Uganda, it was a trip to relish. Unlike many end-of-season club tours in the modern era, the players were thrilled to be there, seeing parts of the world to which only football was ever likely to take them. They were happy on their travels - and would fully prove the point in the following few months.

South African Tour of 1957

May 4 (Johannesburg): *Southern Transvaal 2 Wolves 5* (Murray 5)

May 8 (Pretoria): *Combined Northern and Eastern Transvaal 0 Wolves 1* (Murray)

May 11 (Durban): *Natal 1 Wolves 5* (Broadbent 3, Deeley 2)

May 15 (Cape Town): *Western Province 0 Wolves 6* (Mullen 2, Booth 2, Broadbent, Hooper)

May 18 (Johannesburg): *South Africa X1 1 Wolves 4* (Broadbent 3, Deeley)

May 21 (Johannesburg): *President's X1 3 Wolves 7* (Deeley 2, Murray 2, Mason 2, Showell)

May 24 (Bulawayo): *Southern Rhodesia 1 Wolves 10* (Deeley 3, Mullen 2, Broadbent 2, Murray, Turnbull og, Mason)

May 26 (Kitwe): *Northern Rhodesia 1 Wolves 11* (Mullen 4, Deeley 3, Murray 2, Booth 2)

STARS WITHOUT CARS

There were no Porsches when Wolves ruled the roost. There wasn't even a players' car park worthy of the name. In fact, the young men who were heroes to a generation were often shoulder-to-shoulder with the supporters on the way to and from matches. And a Saturday night dance at the town's Civic Hall, live big bands and all, would usually bring further sightings of several members of Stan Cullis' first team.

Ron Flowers and Peter Broadbent used to walk from their digs for home games and would be accompanied on their way to Molineux by fans of both clubs, visiting supporters stepping off coaches parked near West Park. Even Bert Williams, one of the first Wolves players to own a car, said: "The club frowned on us using bikes because of the danger, so we used to go on the bus.

"At one time, I'd catch one from Bilston and remember having to stand up on occasions. If you had won a game, you could hear the fans afterwards saying: 'We beat them.' If not, it was a case of: 'I see you lost again.' On training days, Jack Davies used to give us a massage with concoctions of various embrocations that smelled awful. The other passengers waiting at the stop weren't too impressed!"

It was the widespread dependence on public transport that prompted an extraordinary line from Cullis before an eagerly-awaited floodlit clash in 1957. "Get the bus in nice and early tonight lads," he ordered. "It's Real Madrid we're playing and there'll be a big crowd."

A spartan means of transport for Wolves' players for a long journey to Sunderland in the early 1950s.

1957-58

Champions Once More

Wolves brought more than just fabulous memories home from South Africa. They also had Cliff Durandt, a Johannesburg-born 17-year-old winger who had represented Transvaal at swimming, rugby and football, and who was accompanied to England that summer by sea in the company of Molineux director James Marshall. And the subject of wingers remained a topic of hot debate as the new season dawned.

Johnny Hancocks was no longer in the squad, nor were the Bradley 'brothers' Bill Shorthouse and Bert Williams, the trio's combined appearance tally for the club standing at 1,174. Change was in the air but Molineux regulars weren't aware of another shock departure in the making.

Harry Hooper's 1956-57 impact had been so marked that he earned an England B game as well as a call-up to the Football League side. He would surely have remained a key man at Molineux had it not been for a disciplinary indiscretion in South Africa. Record price tag and possible England future or not, Stan Cullis once more showed his uncompromising nature with a response that dictated Hooper would not play another competitive match for Wolves, even if there was never any announcement to that effect.

Durandt was seen as one for the longer term despite his promising performance in the pre-season colours v whites game, so the mantel was picked up by Norman Deeley, who was happily available again after his first 31 League games had spanned four seasons. No longer, though, would he - and others - be seen just as stand-ins. "The youngsters will have a fair chance and it's up to them," Cullis said. "They will prove whether we've been right trying to bring along our own players."

Deeley recalls a colours v whites games in which the supposed reserves were leading 6-1 and a halt was called with ten minutes left to prevent the seniors suffering further embarrassment. "It showed the strength

Not ready to hand the baton over yet - and with younger men still in his slipstream!

Billy Wright - always happy to pass on the benefit of his advice, even when en route to 100 England caps.

in depth we had," he said. "Once you were in the side, you were always scared of losing your place because those who were pushing you were so good."

George Showell, Gerry Harris and Bobby Mason, three more players born only a few miles from Wolverhampton, also found opportunity knocking hard. Harris was to play 43 matches that season and Mason 24, although Showell's appearances continued to be sporadic, with Billy Wright and Eddie Stuart still at their peak at centre-half and right-back respectively.

Wolves, who appointed former Preston and Scotland full-back Andy Beattie as a part-time northern-based scout before the campaign kicked off, realised they had to drastically improve their away form. They had lost 12 and won only three of their 21 First Division outings in 1956-57 and the follow-up didn't start encouragingly as they were beaten by the only goal at Everton in front of the day's biggest attendance.

The players who flickered at Goodison came flying out of the blocks at Molineux, though. In a 6.15pm midweek game, they annihilated Bolton 6-1 - their best home start since beating Arsenal in the first League game at Molineux after the war - and added a 5-0 thrashing of Sunderland. Jimmy Murray, having scored four on kick-off day the previous year, led the way with braces in each.

Deeley, who had ended 32 minutes of Bolton resistance with the first goal, also netted in both matches, twice in the first. And inside-forward Colin Booth, preferred to Dennis Wilshaw, was another man on the score-sheet each time. Sunderland were the only side with unbroken membership of the top flight since first joining it and had a fine record at Wolves but their card was marked from the moment they went behind in the third minute.

Deeley superbly scored his fourth goal in four games to salvage a point in the return at Bolton, who missed a controversial twice-taken Edwards penalty. Cullis made his first change at Luton by including Wilshaw on the left wing for Jimmy Mullen - but his goal only partly repaired the damage caused by conceding twice in the first six minutes. The defeat was Wolves' third at the ground in successive seasons.

Nevertheless, a hat-trick in the reserves by Barry Stobart and news that European Cup holders Real Madrid would be visiting Molineux for an October friendly kept morale high. And there was a lower-key development when Wolves beat Walsall 7-2 in the Birmingham League in the first floodlit game to be played at their Castlecroft training headquarters.

Mullen was back with a goal as the first team returned to winning ways, 3-1 at the expense of visiting Blackpool on a day when Booth was absent 24 hours before he was to be married. It was a routine display in which Stuart had one of his best Wolves games - all the more satisfying as it came against the Seasiders' all-South African left-wing combination of Brian Peterson and Bill Perry.

Wolves made it four home victories in a row - seven including the end of the previous season - when Deeley got a late Monday night winner against Aston Villa, Nigel Sims, Peter McParland and all. And when they went to Leicester and recorded their first away success since beating Sunderland on New Year's Day, they were well in the groove.

The second goal in Murray's brace at Filbert Street proved the decider after Eddie Clamp had scored the other from a penalty, the clash being frequently marked by loudspeaker pleas for calm following several controversial refereeing decisions.

Two days later came proof of the different priorities in that era. Harris missed the return at Villa because of his first call from England under-23s, where he linked up with Brian Clough, Jimmy Greaves, Johnny Haynes and Don Howe in a rout of Bulgaria at Chelsea. On the same evening, Wolves overcame the shock of a Wright own goal to also win, Deeley, Murray (his ninth in nine matches) and Broadbent the men on target.

The impressive Deeley had missed the Leicester game with a virus that then ruled keeper Malcolm Finlayson out and handed the more extravagant Noel Dwyer his competitive debut at Villa Park. The unseasonal flu outbreak would affect eight members of the Wanderers camp, including manager Cullis, as well as ruling four Manchester United players out of the trip to face their great rivals at Molineux.

Gerry Harris sees Malcolm Finlayson save in Wolves' 3-1 autumn win over Manchester United. The Reds forward is Johnny Berry, who didn't play again after being badly hurt in the Munich air crash.

Champions United had won the reserve meeting of the clubs on the previous Saturday but that didn't spare them a mauling. They wilted in the face of two goals in the space of five second-half minutes by Deeley and one soon after by Wilshaw, whose drift towards the fringes of the side led to him being linked with both Birmingham and Stoke.

Only Doherty's last-gasp consolation for Matt Busby's men stopped Wolves replacing newly-promoted Nottingham Forest in top spot as Albion's draw with Birmingham made it a Midlands one-two-three at the head of the table.

Then Wolves seized pole position as Tottenham arrived

The big secret behind Wolves' awesome levels of fitness - sheer hard work, as demonstrated by Billy Wright, Eddie Clamp and Eddie Stuart.

for the first League game under Molineux's new floodlights. The previous night match at the ground had kicked off at 5.30pm and Spurs were now left chasing shadows as they crashed 4-0. Wolves hailed the new £25,000 fixtures as the best outside Wembley - a boast they followed with goals by Broadbent (2), Murray and a first of the season from Flowers to make it six straight wins.

Wolves thus eclipsed the best run of the 1953-54 title triumph, and individual highs came, too. Murray was top of the country's scoring lists after ten goals in 11 games and it was no coincidence that the side missed chances in a draw at Leeds in his brief absence through injury. The backlash came via a 5-1 drubbing of Birmingham, two Clamp penalties putting the hosts to the sword.

International calls accompanied Wolves' progress, Flowers joining Bobby Robson and Ronnie Allen in an England B win over a Sheffield combined side. Then Wright won his 86th England cap in a romp in Wales, where Albion right-back Howe, a boyhood Wolves fan and one who eluded Molineux's envied scouting network, was in the squad for the first time.

Wright missed the friendly against Real Madrid and was also absent as Wilshaw and Deeley overturned Chelsea's lead to again bring maximum home points. Wolves' unbeaten League run reached double figures when, after a few days in Whitley Bay, they held on to draw at Newcastle before the players travelled further north to win 3-2 under Hibernian's new lights - a fixture that enabled keeper Finlayson to play in his native country for the first time in ten years.

Murray netted twice in Edinburgh and once for the Football League against the Irish in Belfast later in the week. Wolves' other scorer at Hibs, Clamp, and flu victim Harris both missed the Inter League game, but soon learned that more exciting travels lay just round the corner, Wolves announcing they were to play Belgian champions Anderlecht away at the end of November and visit Real Madrid on December 11.

A moment of concern for (from left) Eddie Stuart, Malcolm Finlayson and Eddie Clamp - but Wolves were almost invincible at Molineux in 1957-58 as they quickly emerged as the team to catch.

Although Wright was part of an England team beaten by Ireland at Wembley at the end of a run of 16 successive victories, there was little to darken the Molineux landscape. When Nottingham Forest were comfortably beaten by first-half goals from Broadbent and Deeley, Wolves had won 11 home matches in a row since losing to Burnley the previous March.

They were still not as convincing away and, with Dwyer embarking on a short run as deputy for the injured Finlayson, they had to be content with a 1-1 draw at Portsmouth, where the equaliser to Clamp's opener came with a first Football League goal from a 19-year-old Irish B forward called Derek Dougan.

Of all teams, it was Albion who broke the Molineux stranglehold with a 1-1 draw. They were undefeated in 13 games, unbeaten away and would have gone joint top had it not been for a Clamp penalty. "Albion matches were always hard," Stuart said. "Ronnie Allen was a great player and lived near us in Tettenhall. I used to give him stick in matches and their fans hated me because I was big and hard. They called me everything!"

Hooper, who had asked for a move after being shunted into the sidelines, made his first senior appearance of the season when Wilshaw was kept out of the trip to Anderlecht by teaching duties. Clubs treated games against prestige opposition in those days more seriously than the big fry regard ties in the Carling Cup and even the FA Cup in the 21st century, and Wolves were unhappy to lose in front of a sell-out 38,000 Brussels crowd to two early goals.

Forever plotting and planning...... Stan Cullis, the man with the job of trying to take the Championship to Molineux for a second time. Such attention to detail was introduced at the club by one of Cullis' close allies, a one-time Wing Commander in the RAF by the name of Charles Reep.

The follow-up, though, was a ringing endorsement of their fitness. Despite arriving seven hours late in Belgium because of fog and then trailing 3-1 with 13 minutes left in front of Manchester City's best crowd of the season by some 10,000, they recovered brilliantly to take the lead through Murray (his second goal of the game), Mason and Broadbent by the 84th minute.

Murray's 13 goals had done more than just drag him level with Deeley at the top of the club's scoring charts. He was also named as reserve for England's 4-0 midweek slaughter of France at Wembley and played for them in a practice match against Tottenham just before.

He stayed in form with one of the goals that beat visiting Burnley in the last game of November, at which point Cullis decided that he could safely cut the Molineux ties of the prolific Wilshaw. Mason and Booth were staking strong enough claims to a place as to prompt the manager to accept a £12,000 bid and allow the senior man to join his native Stoke, who were then managed by former Molineux full-back Frank Taylor.

Wilshaw's stay had been terrific. In another era, he might have doubled his total of 12 senior England caps, especially as they yielded ten goals. Certainly, the statistics suggest he warranted a better crack because, in the early stages of a Wolves stint of 228 games and 113 goals, he also scored twice on his England B debut in Helsinki.

Deeley's rich seam of goals had, by contrast, dried up in the middle of 1957-58 and Cullis had more than one letter telling him it was time he gave an opportunity to Micky Lill. The Essex-born ex-England youth winger did finally get his chance away to title rivals Preston in the first game after Wilshaw's departure but it was in place of the unfit Mullen rather than for Deeley.

Lill had formed a right-flank partnership with Booth in the reserves the previous week. At Deepdale, they teamed up on the left, from where the 21-year-old rid himself of the frustration of two and a half years of waiting by scoring in the first minute. Another goal by Murray ended Preston's ten-game unbeaten run and 16-month undefeated home trot. Lill's belated emergence came as Hooper joined Birmingham for £19,500; alas, the Molineux new boy was to end 1957-58 with the frustrating record of: Played one, scored one.

At the 21-game point, Wolves had the same return as in 1953-54 - 14 wins, five draws, two defeats. They had a slightly inferior goal average but a much bigger lead. Whereas Albion had been level on points in what proved to be the region's proudest football year, the second-placed Baggies now trailed by six points after collapsing at Luton. It was the biggest half-way lead since the war and another four points separated Albion from Preston and Manchester City.

Wolves set off for home by squeezing past Sheffield Wednesday, who became the first away club in the four-month-old season to score more than once at Molineux. In goal for Wednesday as they went bottom of the table courtesy of Clamp's winner was Mike Pinner, an amateur who combined football with life as an articled solicitor and who often caught a cold against Wolves.

An injury to Broadbent before the visit of Everton immediately prior to Christmas made him the last Wolves forward to lose his ever-present record. It gave Slater - confined to the reserves throughout the first half of the season - an opportunity in the inside-forward role he used to occupy for Blackpool. And the side he stepped into extended their lead to eight points with a 2-0 win as Albion lost at Newcastle.

Milestones were coming almost by the week, Wolves' 18th successive game without defeat equalling their longest unbeaten run of 1953-54. Another arrived at Tottenham on Boxing Day, this time an unwanted one as Bobby Smith's early diving header proved to be the only goal. Wolves' first competitive defeat in three and a half months came on the day Flowers lost his 100 per cent record because of flu.

The fixture planners had dealt Wolves an unkind festive hand. After an overnight stay in the

Sadly no longer a part of the playing staff at Wolves by 1957-58 - but Roy Swinbourne was a welcoming host to these youngsters. With him is coach Joe Gardiner.

capital, they set off on the long journey to Sunderland, where they had to do without Wright because of a cut eye from White Hart Lane. Showell was scrambled to the north-east but it was business as usual with goals early in either half from Murray and Broadbent securing a 2-0 win despite Clamp's penalty miss.

Albion's 100 per cent Christmas nevertheless cut the lead to six points by the time attentions switched to the FA Cup. Wolves played poorly at Second Division strugglers Lincoln, where the 25,052 gate still comfortably stands as a club record. The result was hardly in doubt after Mullen scored the only goal because Wolves, for all their attacking arsenal, also had the best defensive record in the top two divisions.

Back in the League, it took an equaliser by Mason to hold visiting Luton while Albion drew at Preston before Wolves headed for Blackpool. Murray and Harris joined their colleagues late after playing for England under-23s against Scotland, the forward remaining for a few extra days at the seaside to provide company for Flowers, who was prescribed a bracing tonic in his fight for fitness after flu.

Murray scored again at Bloomfield Road and Deeley ended his 11-match goal-less streak but neither could prevent a 3-2 defeat against a side inspired by Stanley Matthews. The side's response to seeing Albion trim the gap at the top to four points, though, was a blistering onslaught in both the League and the FA Cup.

A 5-1 fourth-round home win over Portsmouth gave Wolves some further revenge for their shock beating in the 1939 final, Broadbent scoring possibly the best goal of his career with a searing volley to Deeley's corner. Then bottom-of-the-table Leicester, who included Wolverhampton-born Arthur Rowley in their side, were sent packing by the same score.

Wolves, again seven points ahead of Albion after their rivals' hiding at Manchester City, promptly returned to Blackpool, this time in the countdown to their February 8 League clash at Manchester United. Tragically, it was a date United's gifted young side - on their way home from a 3-3 European Cup draw against Red Star Belgrade - were destined not to keep.

"We often stayed at the Norbreck Hotel, even when we were playing somewhere like Old Trafford," Stuart said. "About eight of us were in a restaurant near the tower on the Thursday when a reporter raced in and told us: 'You won't be playing against Manchester United at the weekend. There's been an air disaster.'

"About an hour later, we were going back to the hotel on the tram and passengers openly wept. Although there wasn't much TV in those days, word was getting round by wireless about what had happened. We were very upset. We had good pals on that plane."

The headlines that shocked the world - and caused distressed disbelief in a Wolves squad just about to face Matt Busby's Manchester United.

The teams from the already printed Manchester United v Wolves programme - a publication that never went on sale. Five of the United players died, as did former England keeper Frank Swift, the journalist mentioned in the advert on the left of the page.

United, the title winners in the previous two years, were struggling anyway to complete a hat-trick as they trailed by eight points in the days when there were only two for a win. Stuart added: "I think we would have won the League title whatever because we were being talked of as the best team in the world, not just in our home country. It's questionable to say whether our triumph was devalued by what happened at Munich."

Only fate appeared to decree that Ian Greaves - destined to take charge at Wolves in the early 1980s - was not aboard. He was told to take his bag to the ground in anticipation of him travelling to Belgrade as cover for the injured Roger Byrne. But a late change of mind meant his best mate, Geoff Bent, went instead. "Geoff never came back," Greaves recalls. "I now celebrate two birthdays every year; one on the day of the crash. But for the grace of God, it would have been me there, so I give a thought to the lads each year."

Deeley, who was playing snooker at the Norbreck Hotel when informed by coach Joe Gardiner of the disaster, felt a particular loss. Among the dead was Mark Jones, who had played for England schoolboys alongside him. Through international football, through Dudley-born colossus Duncan Edwards or just through playing against Manchester United, though, most Wolves players had what they regarded as close friends among the 23 dead and many dozen injured.

The tragedy occured on Billy Wright's 34th birthday and Cullis made sure there was an appropriate response. Two days later, at the time his squad should have been running out at Old Trafford, he summoned them into Molineux before a reserve match against Leeds and lined them up on the pitch for three minutes' silence. With flags everywhere flying at half mast, it was described as soccer's saddest Saturday.

A newspaper image of the respectful tribute paid by Wolves' players at Molineux on the day they should have been at Old Trafford.

The reaction was panicky. One columnist questioned whether football teams should fly because of the 'ever-present risk of a similar occurrence' while Football League officials felt they had more ammunition in their already firm resistance to the concept of the European Cup. The following week, Eintracht Frankfurt took their players on two planes for a game at Arsenal, Nottingham Forest following suit when they played in Fiorentina.

Public confidence in air travel was not helped shortly afterwards when, two days before Wolves were to play a Cup tie at Bolton, a plane crashed in the Lancashire town and killed 34. No wonder the Molineux youngsters were happy to undergo a tiring 36-hour trip by land to a youth tournament in Germany at the end of the season.

Although United's fixtures were disrupted, football returned to normal as soon as possible. As if to underline the point, bookies made United a 100/9 bet to win the FA Cup from 9/4 and installed Wolves as new favourites at 2/1 - a tag that sat very comfortably when Darlington, backed by 11 train-loads of supporters, were despatched 6-1 after a shock victory over Chelsea in round three.

The tie was watched by more than 55,000 and was effectively settled by a Murray hat-trick. It was followed by a 3-2 home win over Leeds that restored the team's lead to five points, with Preston now second, Luton third and Albion fourth. A Birmingham side containing Harry Hooper were then hammered 5-1 by Wolves for the second time in the season, Murray scoring his second hat-trick on successive Saturdays and Deeley netting twice to take his tally to five in four League games.

Wolves had played five consecutive home matches since losing at Blackpool and registered wins of 5-1, 5-1, 6-1, 3-2 and 5-1; that's 24 goals at virtually five a game in three days short of a month. Slater had played in the first three of them before ten minutes of heading practice at Birmingham University brought on a back strain that ruled him out of the FA Cup sixth-round clash at Bolton.

Despite the proximity of a second League title in five seasons, the FA Cup remained special for Wolves fans and no fewer than 15,000 travelled to a tie for which the hosts said they could have sold 100,000 tickets. There was to be no happy return down the A41, though, despite Mason's third Cup goal of the season. One of Bolton's two came from England under-23 international Dennis Stevens, Dudley-born cousin of Duncan Edwards.

Cullis found himself linked with the Newcastle manager's job shortly before the clash of the clubs at a snow-bound

Eddie Stuart covers as Malcolm Finlayson gathers during Wolves' emphatic FA Cup victory over Darlington.

Two snow showers fell in Wolves' clash with Newcastle on March 8. But the table-toppers were not put off by the winter wonderland and won 3-1.

Molineux - one of two League matches Slater also missed - but nothing else changed. Wolves had Welshman Ron Howells - the son of a rugby union international - at wing-half in one of only two appearances he made that season, the team scoring twice in the last 15 minutes to win 3-1.

When Wolves won 2-1 in a rearranged midweek game at Chelsea three days later, they were again seven points clear and goals were coming from familiar and unfamiliar sources. Deeley netted for the sixth League game running and Showell - at left-back for the rested Harris - volleyed a late winner at a time when he was playing on the right wing because of concussion.

Cullis lowered his cautious guard to admit: "The League Championship is now within our grasp." But his sense of anticipation didn't stop him strengthening his squad by signing Scottish international forward Jackie Henderson from Portsmouth. "It would be a shame to lose it merely for the sake of an experienced forward," he added.

The 26-year-old started in the reserves as the established guard continued to blaze their golden trail, Murray scoring his third hat-trick in a month - including two diving headers - as Wolves burned Nottingham Forest off in the second half at the City Ground.

A week later came the clash of the division's highest-scoring teams, Wolves and Manchester City. And the 3-3 draw, containing an own goal at either end and a penalty miss by Deeley, meant the home side had gone a full year without a Molineux defeat in any competition - a feat they had last achieved in 1955.

International managers and selectors did not have the sensitivities of club bosses to concern them five decades ago, so Wright and Clamp from one camp and Howe, Allen and Kevan from the other were named for the Football League side to face the Scottish League at Newcastle only four days before an Albion v Wolves meeting that took on historic proportions.

The derby, so vital to the destiny of the Championship, was the first League game ever to be made all-ticket and 56,904 packed into The Hawthorns. Arsenal were the only visiting side to have won there that season but Wolves simply blew their hosts away with a brilliant 3-0 victory, Murray scoring twice in the second half to take his season's total into the 30s.

Cullis missed the slaughter with a virus that later saw him packed off to the West Country for revitalisation but Wolves went into Easter with a six-point lead that Preston cut to four (from one more match played) by winning at Blackpool on Good Friday. Albion were nine off the pace, from two extra matches, after drawing at Spurs.

Only twice in 39 League and Cup matches had Wolves failed to score but they were happy to manage just one - a fearsome Clamp penalty - to edge past Portsmouth at Molineux on a Saturday afternoon on which Wright was said by the Express & Star correspondent 'Commentator' to have reduced the promising Dougan to 'ordinary proportions.'

Flowers, hardly seen since his Christmas illness, came back in for Slater at Arsenal on the Monday afternoon, the heat having been turned up a shade by Preston's morning win over Blackpool. North End, who still had to visit Molineux, had won 17 of 19 games at home, where only Wolves had beaten them, and had drawn at Manchester United on the Saturday.

Burton-on-Trent teenager Allan Jackson made his Wolves debut on the left wing at Highbury and set up Broadbent to open the scoring. Herd then shot well wide from a controversial penalty before Murray hit the killer second. It looked all over bar the shouting, only for the Gunners to throw a spanner into the works by deservedly winning at Molineux 24 hours later, Wright conceding a second and this time converted penalty in two days.

Wolves were still five points clear when the FA left them with mixed emotions prior to England's first game since the Munich disaster. Following the deaths of Edwards, Tommy Taylor and Roger Byrne, the selectors named Slater - three and a half years after he won his only two previous caps - alongside Wright.

Despite Molineux satisfaction at his inclusion to face Scotland at Hampden, there was concern that he and his club and country captain would miss the League game at home to Preston. It was the clash between first place and second, although it would become relatively academic if Wolves won at Burnley in the meantime and Villa did well against Preston.

Injury kept Wright, Slater and Mason out at Turf Moor, with Showell, Flowers and Booth returning. Clamp's penalty opened the scoring but Burnley, having done the double against

Malcolm Finlayson saves bravely from Arsenal's Gordon Nutt at Highbury - and missed only five games in Wolves' triumphant 1957-58 campaign.

Wolves the previous season, equalised and had a goal disallowed in a 1-1 draw while Villa did their bit for the West Midlands cause by drawing at Deepdale.

The issue was thus kept open for another week before Cullis' men saw off Preston, their 2-0 home win over their nearest rivals including a late own goal by Gordon Milne. The visitors were without their star turn, Tom Finney, because of England commitments but the final margin of five points, with Tottenham and Albion well back in third and fourth, left no room for argument.

Wolves proved what worthy champions they were two days later after the bond between they and Manchester United was underlined. One of the first congratulatory telegrams was from the recuperating Matt Busby, whose players formed a guard of honour to welcome Wolves on to the pitch before the rearranged game at Old Trafford. The visitors then showed their appreciation by winning 4-0!

Murray finished with 32 goals despite not scoring in the last five matches, Deeley 23 and Broadbent 21 while Clamp and Mason were also in double figures. Wolves totalled 103 goals - the first time they had reached a Division One century - and had as many points as any top-flight side since the war. Only a last-day defeat at Sheffield Wednesday prevented them equalling Arsenal's all-time record points haul of 66.

They also won the Central League, Birmingham League, Worcestershire Combination, Worcestershire Combination Cup and FA Youth Cup. Typically, though, Cullis was not satisfied - after all, the FA Cup had eluded them! "I am very proud and have never seen players work so hard," he said. "But I've got to graft some steadiness on to my team. It was also that shortcoming that lost us the quarter-final at Bolton."

Jimmy Murray finds himself well outnumbered in this Wolves attack against Preston - but Wolves were not to be denied the win that made them champions in style.

Even before being crowned champions for the second time, Wolves had a flood of offers to go abroad in the summer. From a choice that included Spain, Holland, Germany, Switzerland, Italy, Sweden, Gibraltar, Malta and Denmark, they eventually settled on a three-country trip taking in individual games in Stuttgart and Zurich and then a prestigious four-team tournament in Brussels.

Their fortunes were surprisingly mixed. They scored four apiece in beating Stuttgart and Grasshoppers but were trounced by Anderlecht, Juventus and Beerschott in the competition staged at the Heysel Stadium. "It was a humiliating experience," Finlayson said. Another example of the pride Cullis and his men felt, wherever and whoever they were playing…..

There was good reason for the collapse in Belgium. At the end of a season in which Molineux youngster Les Cocker played 11 times for England youths, Harris was named for England under-23s and Clamp, Wright, Slater and Broadbent were away at the World Cup finals in Sweden. Hand in hand with club glories came such personal highlights.

Once more, though, the national side disappointed on the biggest stage of all. Having won 4-0 away to Scotland in Slater's comeback on the spring day on which Munich survivor Bobby Charlton scored in the first of his 106 senior internationals, they had contrasting warm-up results with the Wolves part-timer in the side alongside Wright. They beat Portugal at Wembley but were then annihilated by Yugoslavia in Belgrade.

But the trip to Scandinavia spelled letdown - for club and country captain Wright in particular. At the age of 34, he knew his last World Cup opportunity had come and gone. Any future silverware would have to come at club level - but at least there was a decent chance of that at Molineux.

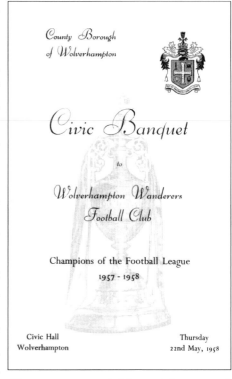

Close-season activities at home and abroad - all the way from the Civic Hall to the Belgian capital||!

INTERNATIONAL HONOURS

Of Wolves And England

Stan Cullis had mixed views about his players playing for England. Although patriotic and proud - he himself represented his country 12 times in official matches - he was known to remind them not to play 'the England way' back in the hurly-burly of the First Division.

All of which left him with a potential headache after his club provided the national side with an entire half-back line in the 1958 World Cup finals in Sweden! Billy Wright was still going strong, his total of caps having climbed into the 90s by the time a squad weakened by the Munich tragedy left home soil. But alongside him were relative newcomers Bill Slater and Eddie Clamp.

Slater had played only 14 matches in the club's second title triumph and spent much of the season in the shadow of Ron Flowers before getting the nod from the selectors at the expense of his Molineux colleague. He had not played for England since facing West Germany in December, 1954 but was clearly a thinker on the game. Several years earlier, he wrote an article extolling the virtues of the Hungarians, having seen them close up when he represented his country as an amateur in the 1952 Helsinki Olympics. He pointed out their major strengths in an FA magazine but laments: "Probably no-one took any notice." Many of the same Magyar players were present when they then thrashed England home and away.

Clamp's elevation had been more orthodox, via the England Boys team and Young England. Not that there was much ordinariness about his play. He was one of the first players to take the ball to the corner flag to kill time. He was a good long passer as well and, from the kick-off, he or Flowers would sometimes hit the ball straight out for a throw near one of the corner flags to immediately get opponents on the back foot and the crowd lifted.

Clamp also perfected the art of

Billy Wright lines up before the match against Uruguay in Montevideo that brought him England cap no 50. Now time was running out for him at international level.

Air time for Bill Slater with Wolves secretary Jack Howley (top) and director Arthur Oakley (seated).

jumping off the bus and then walking up Molineux Alley to arrive at 2.50pm on match-days, leaving Cullis pulling out what remained of his hair!

No-one would ever have called Clamp an angel yet, on debut-day at Manchester United back in 1954, his mum - the popular laundry lady at Molineux for decades - said to a senior player: "You will look after my Eddie, won't you?"

Even at that juncture, the Wolves dressing room knew that a young man built in the gangly Tom Galley mould would need no special minding. But there was more to him than brawn. "He had this hard-man reputation," said Ted Farmer. "Chopper Clamp they called him. But he was a terrific player. I recall him having a great game at Spurs against their best-ever side."

Eddie Stuart, who later played alongside Clamp at Stoke as well, also recalls the iron-man image affectionately. "It was said that if Eddie Clamp missed a player on the way through, Eddie Stuart got him instead. But Eddie had real talent. He hadn't had a good game unless he pushed the ball through an opponent's legs at some point and came out with it the other side!"

Unlike Slater, Clamp had been a virtual Wolves ever-present in 1957-58, playing 45 games out of 46 - three more even than Wright - in League and Cup. He peaked at just the right time for the World Cup because he didn't make his England debut until accompanying his two club colleagues in the 1-1 draw with USSR in Moscow's Lenin Stadium only three weeks before the tournament.

The same nation were the first opponents for unchanged England in the championships, Wolves thus having the honour of providing the country's half-back line on the highest stage. The trio did enough in a 2-2 draw in Gothenburg to keep their places for the deadlock with Brazil - the only time the eventual winners failed to score - and Wright later revealed that Slater bruised the inside of his knees as he kept banging them together to stop the gifted Didi slipping the ball between his legs! The wing-half was fit enough, though, to remain in harness with his club colleagues in a 2-2 draw with Austria in Boras that sent England into a play-off against USSR back in Gothenburg.

This time, Ronnie Clayton was preferred to Clamp but failed to stave off a 1-0 defeat in a game in which England lacked the firepower to beat Wolves' mid-1950s adversary, Lev Yashin. The decider against USSR was a bitter-sweet occasion at Molineux, marking the end of Clamp's brief career at full international level but launching that of Broadbent.

The Golden Wolf Cubs

The FA Youth Cup was a big deal for Wolverhampton Wanderers in the 1950s. At a time when the home production of players was considerably more prevalent in the game than today, they reached the final three times - twice playing against Manchester United - and ensured that the intense friendly rivalry between Molineux and Old Trafford was not confined to first-team level.

Wolves advanced to the last stage for the first time in 1952-53, the season of the competition's inauguration, with West Brom, Birmingham and none other than Huntley & Palmers among their conquests before they lost heavily to United in the two-leg final.

Undeterred, they soon launched a fresh bid to lift a trophy Stan Cullis held in high regard. They blazed another thrilling trail in 1953-54, scoring 26 goals in brushing aside Stoke, Derby and Spalding in the opening three rounds, Joe Bonson netting five times against Derby and four against Spalding. After Nottingham Forest and Portsmouth had then been edged out, Wolves cut loose again to hammer West Ham 8-2 over the two legs of the semi-final, a crowd of over 21,000 watching their 6-1 win in the home game.

United again proved a step too far, though, after overpowering Albion 7-1 in the other semi-final. Wolves shocked an 18,246 Old Trafford crowd by leading 3-1 at half-time in the away first leg but were pegged back to 4-4 by a side containing Eddie Colman, Wilf McGuinness, Bobby Charlton, David Pegg, Albert Scanlon and the two-goal Duncan Edwards.

A bumper 28,651 crowd turned up for the

Wolves' players, led by Micky Lill, touch down in Europe on their summer tour. Back home, the young pretenders were out for glory of their own.

return on the night Billy Wright was presented with the League Championship trophy, only for the masses to be disappointed when Edwards' harrying prompted a harsh hand-ball decision that allowed Pegg - twice on target at Old Trafford - to score the only goal of the night.

United went on to win the cup in each of its first five years while Wolves suffered a relative dip in their fortunes before regrouping and coming back strong in 1957-58. They collected a quartet of Midlands scalps by beating Albion, Aston Villa, Stoke and Leicester but were taken to the third replay of their run when a 1-1 draw at home to Bolton set up an unusual double date at Burnden Park on April 16, 1958.

In the afternoon, Wolves' reserves, needing a point to lift the Central League title for the fourth time since the war, left nothing to chance with a 3-2 win. Then the stage was cleared for the youngsters to take the club into the semi-final of the FA Youth Cup once more with a 3-1 victory under lights secured by two goals from Cliff Durandt and one from Brian Perry.

This time United awaited them in the last four and were thankful to escape with a first-leg draw in front of 16,500 at Old Trafford. A side containing Nobby Stiles, Johnny Giles, and David Gaskill, equalised in injury-time after Ted Farmer, who had scored 86 goals in the club's junior teams the previous season, netted just before half-time.

United also drew first blood in a return watched by 14,500 at Molineux 48 hours later. Wolves skipper Granville Palin missed a penalty but Farmer shook off the after-effects of shingles and Asian flu to head home a 49th minute cross from Des Horne, who then made it 2-1 with a rocket shot ten minutes from the end. Gerry Mannion added a third and Wolves had ended the Reds' long domination of the competition.

Wolves' 1958 FA Youth Cup winners. Back row from left: Jack Screen (trainer), Gordon Yates, Gerry Mannion, Granville Palin (captain), John Cullen, Tony Corbett, John Kirkham, Bill Shorthouse (coach). Front row: David Read, Brian Perry, Phil Kelly, Stan Cullis, Cliff Durandt, Des Horne, Ted Farmer. Ian Hall and Les Cocker also played in both legs of the final but aren't on the photograph.

In the final, they shocked a crowd of 19,621 when they took the lead through Perry at Chelsea, 6-2 victors over Arsenal in the semi-final. But a team including Jimmy Greaves, under-23 international centre-half Mel Scott and six other players of first-team experience subjected Wolves to the pummelling of their young lives as they turned a 1-0 deficit into a 5-1 win.

Greaves, who had also scored in a first-team clash of the clubs that season, was nevertheless told by Durandt after the game: "We're not out of it." And Wolves coach Bill Shorthouse, having waved Cullis off on tour to Switzerland after the manager had watched the first leg, was glowing with pride as Wolves ran amok in the return to lead 4-0 at half-time, Farmer scoring them all.

Such was the excitement and mayhem that Phil Kelly motioned to go out for the second half with his shirt on back to front. But relative calm was restored and the gap was extended to six on the night through a brace by Durandt before Greaves struck to set up a tense finale. Wolves hung on and sensationally won 6-1 to take the cup 7-6 on aggregate.

"We couldn't get hold of the ball and were given a salutary lesson," Greaves recalled. "We thought we only had to turn up to win. Their players had a mental strength, character and determination our team lacked - and I include myself in that." Chelsea coach Dickie Foss merely said to his players: "It was only half-time but you buggers thought you had won it. Never go out on a football pitch with your big heads on."

Farmer later boarded the no 58 bus for his Dudley home, offered his 11d fare and was told by the conductor: "You'll never have to pay on my bus after what you've done tonight." The striker, later cruelly cut down by injury when first-team and international stardom beckoned, recalls: "We had a great team spirit and the spectators wanted it so badly after seeing us go close a few times.

"We were hammered at Stamford Bridge and, although we were convinced we'd win the second leg, I don't think any of us really thought we were going to win the tie. I swear the crowd was quite small at kick-off but the cheers as each goal went in were heard round the town and another thousand or two came in to have a look. Eventually, there were over 17,000 present!

"The first team had won everything that season and this was the very last match of the season, so it was the icing on the cake. The FA Youth Cup win was the highlight of my career because it seemed more than just football - it was for the pride of the town."

The man who laid the foundations for Wolves in the art of youth development - Major Frank Buckley, club manager from 1927 to 1944.

1958-59

A Victorious Defence

Stan Cullis had little truck with the critics - often from London - who considered Wolves' style of play to be unsophisticated. In his eyes, a move of five or six passes was a move that had more chance of breaking down before it reached the telling area close to the opposition goal. So he encouraged his players to get the ball forward much more quickly.

Often, it was through the brilliant wingers the club had at their disposal in the 1940s and 1950s but the manager wasn't averse to the occasional big boot down-field and it wasn't unheard of for Wolves to launch the ball rugby-style into touch deep in the other half just to gain some ground and impetus. It wasn't always pretty but it was highly effective and entertaining.

With a second title in the bag, Cullis had every justification for his methods and Wolves started 1958-59 in the style to which they were accustomed. They put five past Nottingham Forest on the day Des Horne - a South African left-winger signed more than 18 months earlier - made his debut

Wolves line up before their 1958-59 campaign with the handsome array of six trophies that they had gathered at various levels the previous season.

but followed up with a defeat at newly-promoted West Ham in the first top-flight game to be staged at Upton Park for 26 years.

Then they crashed 6-2 at Stamford Bridge, where Jimmy Greaves, who claims Chelsea boss Ted Drake did not like Cullis, scored five goals and had another disallowed. Although the visitors went ahead through Bobby Mason, their defending had Cullis struggling to keep a lid on his anger at half-time. "Right, gentleman," he said as he shut the dressing room door behind him, "we've been playing for 45 minutes and I wondered how much longer it will be before any of you deign to tackle their number 10."

Greaves, who called Wolves 'a real class act,' was to punish them with another hat-trick in 1960-61. He used finesse rather than brawn and would dink or stroke the ball home rather than hammer it - information that Malcolm Finlayson happily imparted to his former team-mate Nigel Sims when Wolves' players shared a train home with the Aston Villa side hammered 7-2 at West Ham on the same day in August, 1958.

"I passed on what advice I could to Nigel," Finlayson recalls. "Chelsea were due to take on Villa pretty soon afterwards down at Stamford Bridge and I wanted to help him. Jimmy, who was still a newcomer, had embarrassed me by rolling the ball in gently and I told Nigel to be wary of that ability. As keepers go, he was not short of confidence and thought he'd have the answers. But, if I remember right, Greavesie stuck a couple past him as well!"

They didn't do it for the money! A 1959 contract shows Eddie Stuart earned £20 a week with England's top club.

Wolves drew their return against West Ham in front of a second successive 50,000-plus crowd at Molineux and then embarked on a run of four wins. In the one at Blackburn, though, Cullis was on the receiving end of bizarre allegations from three women that he had been heard swearing from the touchline - bizarre, because everyone who knew him was aware he never swore.

The quartet of victories also contained an emphatic double over Villa, Sims and all, which prompted the retired Bert Williams to describe Eddie Stuart and Gerry Harris as the best all-time Wolves full-back pairing; a suitable endorsement of form that was to remain at a very high level.

Surprisingly, Jimmy Murray's 32 goals in 1957-58 hadn't earned him a place at the start of the season, his dip in fortunes letting in Jackie Henderson. The Scot didn't deliver goals until he was switched to the left wing, though - and then only three of them. He and the recalled Murray scored braces against Villa, only for Wolves to lose to Newcastle and Tottenham and slip to ninth. At Spurs, Bill Slater netted and missed with a three-times-taken penalty from which Clamp finally scored.

Defeat at White Hart Lane in late September meant Wolves slipped to ninth in their defence of the League title.

The latter did likewise in a terrific 4-0 home win over Manchester United in early October as Cliff Durandt made his debut in the first game ever staged by the club on a Saturday night. It was a visionary move but, with TV pulling out of planned live screening, the experiment was deemed to have failed with only 36,840 turning up, although the loss of Billy Wright, Peter Broadbent, Bobby Charlton, Wilf McGuinness and Harry Gregg to the Ireland v England match was also a factor.

The Molineux duo were back as Wolves crashed 4-1 in the Charity Shield at Bolton, where Gerry Mannion made his debut and Durandt scored in his second game. League fortunes remained high, even when George Showell was tried as a makeshift striker for four games. He scored the point-saver at Arsenal, where Broadbent played his 250th League match and Wolves became the first visiting team in 1958-59 to avoid defeat. Then he netted in a home win over Birmingham, who were hit by a brace from Jimmy Mullen - the recent recipient of a £1,000 benefit cheque.

At the other end, Finlayson was again proving his worth despite being carried off unconscious at home to Manchester City and forcing Murray to play as emergency keeper. Finlayson played 37 First Division matches in the 1957-58 triumph and would figure in 39 out of 42 this time round. He was a key component in the success in the wake of Williams' retirement and was delighted to repay Cullis' faith. "Stan was a hero of mine from the day my father took me to Hampden," he said.

"I was ten and disappointed Scotland lost 4-0 to the England side Stan was captaining. But he was so impressive that I respected and admired him greatly from then onwards. I think it's an absolute disgrace that he has not been honoured and recognised in the same way that other great managers like Jock Stein, Bill Shankly, Matt Busby and Bill Nicholson have been."

Some Molineux sources thought Finlayson was going to play for Scotland against Wales in October, 1958 but Blackpool's George Farm was picked instead. "It would have been lovely to play for Scotland but coming to England and enjoying a successful career has made the loss of a possible international career a sacrifice worth making," he said. "Stan repeatedly recommended me for a cap but it was not easy for Anglos to get into the Scottish side at that time.

"It was picked by a committee of selectors and there was a heavy Rangers and Celtic influence. I once said at a dinner in Scotland, to a hiss of dismay, that I wouldn't have swapped my Wolves career for one with my country. How could I say anything else after winning the League twice and the FA Cup once down here? And I played well over 200 Millwall games before that."

Stuart, one of the first overlapping full-backs, also found international football a case of so near yet so far. He impressed the selectors on one of Wolves' visits to Scotland and heard the next day that he'd been selected in the 15 for a match against Wales. But the link turned to anti-climax, as did reports that he was to join Ron Flowers in a Europe side to face Real Madrid in a fixture that was eventually blocked by FIFA.

"I had strong Scottish connections because a lot of Stuarts had come from the Inverness area," he said. "I was delighted to be named. Scotland were a good side then - there wasn't much between them and England - and I'd love to have played for them. But, although my grandfather had been born in Scotland, my father was from South Africa, so it was decided I wasn't eligible.

"When I left for England in 1951, my mother said to me in Afrikaans: 'I hope you'll always stay South African and don't change your nationality.' I did switch to British citizenship in the 1960s or 1970s and it rankles now that if I'd changed earlier, I could have played for Scotland. International football in South Africa at the time wasn't a big thing because of the apartheid problems. Many countries wouldn't play South Africa."

While Slater was recalled for England in their partial-revenge Wembley slaughter of the USSR,

Eddie Stuart and Malcolm Finlayson remained uncapped but Wolves still had a big say with England. In this 1958 get-together are Eddie Clamp (fourth from left, back row), Bill Slater (third from left, front row), Billy Wright (fourth from left, front row) and Peter Broadbent (one in from right, front row).

Stuart had to be content with performing his heroics only at club level and his impressive contribution had been extended to 50 consecutive appearances by the time Wolves went Continental themselves by making their debut in the European Cup. Alas, the experience was not as fulfilling as it had been hoped. The side recovered well from a defeat at Albion with a win over Preston, Mason scoring both goals, but a brace from Broadbent could earn only a 2-2 home draw with Schalke.

Geoff Sidebottom, another Wath Wanderers product, replaced the injured Finlayson in all three of those games and at Burnley as Wolves pinched maximum points, scorer Allan Jackson becoming the fourth player in the three-month-old campaign to play at no 9.

Finlayson, as a Millwall player, had been a travelling reserve when London played in Basle in 1955 in the forerunner of the UEFA Cup, the Inter Cities Fairs Cup. He duly made his European Cup debut in the return against Schalke in West Germany but neither he at one end

Eddie Stuart, stand-in skipper for Billy Wright, leads Wolves out, followed by goalkeeper Malcolm Finlayson.

nor Jackson's second senior goal at the other could stave off a 2-1 defeat and an aggregate 4-3 exit.

Wolves wobbled as they beat Luton and Everton but lost to Bolton and suffered their first defeat at Leicester since the 1920s. Cullis recalled Murray for Jackson, then demoted the senior man again to give Broadbent a six-game run at centre-forward. He scored in a reviving win at Nottingham Forest and figured strongly in a spectacular Christmas double - one of no fewer than 11 the club recorded that season.

He netted a Boxing Day hat-trick at Portsmouth, where Wolves won 5-3 despite having been 3-1 down with half an hour to go against a side just thrashed 6-0 at West Ham. But he failed to make the score-sheet the following day when Pompey were trounced 7-0 at Molineux, Deeley and Colin Booth each scoring hat-tricks and five of the goals coming in 16 second-half minutes.

Chelsea kicked off 1959 by becoming the only club that season to do the double over Wolves, whose response was to give right-winger Micky Lill another opportunity. The lively Londoner scored in the 4-2 FA Cup third-round win at frosty Barrow - then members of the Football League - and, although on the sidelines again for the Cup knock-out in the snow against visiting Bolton, was recalled for the pivotal home game against Blackburn on January 31.

Wolves under pressure in their FA Cup fourth-round exit against Bolton at a wintry Molineux in late January, 1959. Left: Eddie Stuart slides in to challenge the fearsome Nat Lofthouse while, right, keeper Malcolm Finlayson merges with the ball, although not without a little discomfort.

Cullis ditched the idea of squeezing square pegs into round holes and restored Murray at no 9 in the season's 16th forward-line combination. The one-time England challenger had scored only five goals to date but joined Lill, Mason (2) and Deeley - by now on the left wing - in destroying Rovers 5-0. And Murray clicked by netting another 15 times as an ever-present from then on.

He scored in the shadow of Mason's latest brace in a thrilling 4-3 win at Newcastle and joined Broadbent and Deeley as two-goal men in a 6-2 Molineux annihilation of Leeds. Leaders Wolves had hit 32 goals in seven League matches and weren't even checked by a defeat at Old Trafford, where Charlton's last-gasp strike took Manchester United's golden run to 23 points out of 24 and lifted them level at the top. Wolves were back in Manchester a week later and tamed City 4-1.

Cullis' men put six past a title-chasing Arsenal side containing John Barnwell and Tommy Docherty and took their usual St Andrew's toll of Birmingham before Albion were slammed 5-2 at Molineux, Lill becoming the fifth player from the club to score a 1958-59 hat-trick. Lill then netted both goals in a win at Preston when Wolves' settled defence were weakened by the loss of Stuart - a development that brought a rare opportunity for Welshman Gwynfor Jones.

The powerful Stuart had been struck in the left eye by the ball in training and was in hospital, ordered not to move a muscle, as the champions impressed at Deepdale and stayed on course for a successful title defence. He had played 68 consecutive games in a superb rearguard who perhaps didn't get the credit they deserved behind a pacy and generally free-scoring attack.

If there was a criticism of the defenders, it was that they weren't weighing in with goals. But Clamp, who, like Slater, had to be content with playing only two-thirds of Wolves' League games while fellow wing-half Flowers played almost three-quarters of them, took a small step towards addressing that with one of the three in a comfortable Easter win at Leeds. Harris then did likewise in the follow-up home draw against Burnley.

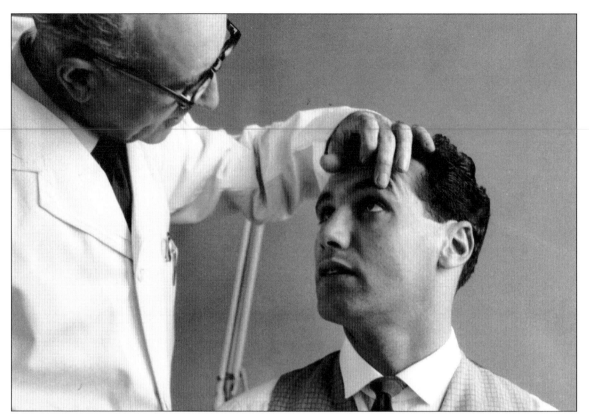

I'm all right to play, honest! Eddie Stuart is given a once-over by the long-serving George Palmer after injuring his left eye in training.

Phil Kelly made his debut at right-back in the 2-2 draw at Bolton - an improvement on three defeats that season at the hands of those other Wanderers. With Wright away playing in the victory over Scotland in the company of Broadbent and Flowers and becoming the first man in the world to win 100 caps, Clamp was captain for the first time on the night Booth hit the club's 100th League goal of another memorable season. But the international trio soon rejoined the charge for the finishing line.

They helped ten-man Wolves end the top flight's last unbeaten home record at Blackpool two nights later, Stuart having a terrific game against his countryman Bill Perry after bravely declaring himself fit to play against doctor's orders. Incredibly, Mason suffered an identical injury in the first half at Bloomfield Road and played no further part either in a game then still locked at 0-0 or for the rest of the 1958-59 campaign.

Wolves were two points clear of United with a game in hand and a much superior goal average. They knew a win at home to Luton five days later could be enough to secure the championship and win they duly did, by 5-0 no less. United's victory on the same

> **CAUGHT SHORT**
> Bill Slater once had to replace his torn shorts in full view of a 100,000-plus crowd at a Scotland v England game at Hampden Park. There were wolf whistles and much worse from the amused Scots but the player insists it was a lot of fuss over such a small thing. "It was a very cold day," he recalls. "In fact, I'd say it was a shrivellingly cold day."

afternoon kept the issue open, mathematically, but a congratulatory telegram from Old Trafford within half an hour of the final whistle at Molineux confirmed that the battle was over to all intents and purposes.

Leicester players applauded Wolves on to the field four nights later, so obvious was it where the title was destined for. Then the visitors kept the game tight for 67 minutes until Deeley - just named for the England summer tour of the Americas - scored the 19th goal of his tremendous personal contribution. Lill, with goal no 13 in only his 19th game, and Murray added others, and the hordes swarmed on to the pitch in celebration.

It fell to the Leicester chairman Len Shipman - a Football League management committee member - to present the trophy to Wright. Little did fans know of the momentous announcement the skipper would make four months later. A groin injury meant he missed the last-day win at Everton, where Murray scored for the seventh match in a row, so he had played his final competitive game for the club.

So had much-loved Geordie boy Jimmy Mullen, whose outing in the 1-1 home draw against Tottenham in March was the last of a magnificent stay

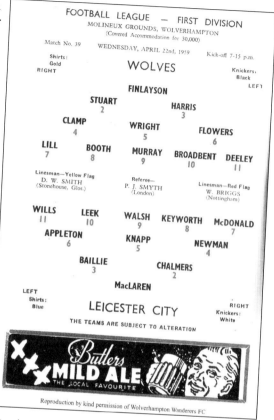

comprising 486 matches in League and cups and no fewer than 112 goals, 99 of the latter in the First Division. He had played 16 games in the successful title defence and, fittingly in view of his many floodlit outings, had also appeared in the club's European Cup bow.

Wolves, with a club record 13 away League wins, headed United by six points as they won their third title in six years. Old Trafford boss Matt Busby said: "They stood for everything good in British football. They played with great power, spirit and style. Stan Cullis moulded his teams in his own image. They were honest, straightforward, uncomplicated and full of determination and zest."

Murray's heroics over the last three months had again made him Wolves' leading Division One scorer with 21, although Broadbent was one ahead in all competitions. The side's tally of 110 goals was easily a Molineux record in the top flight, no fewer than 71 of them coming after the mid-point of the 42-game campaign. Remarkably, they had averaged well over three goals a match over their last 17 League fixtures. And their tally of 11 doubles equalled a national post-war record.

Despite losing three more times than 12 months earlier, Wolves also had the best defensive record with only 49 goals against, so their crown sat very comfortably. As if that wasn't enough, they won their fifth Central League title of the 1950s (by 15 points) to equal the all-time English record of six - and were Birmingham League champions for good measure. It had been another quite magnificent season.

1959-60

So Close To The Double

Like all good things, it had to end one day. But not many expected the big announcement to come in the manner it did. Billy Wright, having been away on an England tour in the summer of 1959 and then gone through the pre-season slog for fitness back home, chose Molineux's traditional curtain-raiser fixture as the day to end his exemplary Molineux career.

The official line is that Wright called time when younger colleagues dashed past him on the training runs that Stan Cullis and Joe Gardiner supervised over Cannock Chase - punishing sessions that often made players physically sick. He was also influenced by a former Home Secretary, who told him to beware the temptation of going on one year too many. But there was a prompt from inside Molineux as well.

Towards the end of Wright's fabulous Wolves stay of 541 League and Cup games, the claims

Domestic bliss! Billy Wright in his new role as time is about to be called on his superb playing career.

of George Showell to become more than just his occasional deputy had increased in strength. The Bradley boy made his debut back in 1955 and would have waltzed into most top-flight teams but had still not totalled 50 League appearances by the end of 1958-59. He had been terrific as Wright's replacement in the home game with Real Madrid, though, and couldn't be expected to stay a reserve much longer.

He played well in convincing victories in Zurich and Nuremburg on Wolves' end-of-season travels while Wright didn't have a good press on the England summer tour. Maybe, just maybe, Billy feared he would be in the Central League side if he carried on playing.

Eddie Stuart with Tommy McMullan, Des Horne and Cliff Durandt.

Whatever the thinking, the big announcement came on Friday, August 7 and was relegated to three paragraphs on the front of the Express & Star by the disclosure at the same time that the Queen was expecting her third child.

In a much fuller version of the story on the back page, though, Wright, who had told Showell of his intentions beforehand, said: "I've had a wonderful run with a wonderful club but this is it. I want to finish while I'm still at the top. I reckon I was good for another season at least but, since I got my 100th cap and my CBE, I have thought it over and decided this is the time to make way."

As the younger man pledged to try to do justice to the shirt he was taking on, there weren't any great shockwaves among his team-mates. "The rumours had been flying round the dressing room because we knew Billy's time in the first team was coming towards a close," says Ted Farmer. "We weren't shocked but we had so much admiration for him and he was never pushy. He led by example on and off the pitch."

Wright, described by Stan Cullis as 'the best example of a professional footballer I have ever seen,' was named in the whites side for the following day's annual friendly against the colours (the first team). But, as a lovely touch, the manager switched him to a gold shirt at the last minute to protect his record of never having played for Wolves reserves.

An attendance of more than 20,000 - twice the norm for a fixture from which the proceeds went to charity - turned up to see him marking Farmer in the whites' 4-2 win. A famous era had ended, although Wright had been told there was a job for life for him at Molineux if he wanted one. Cullis favoured giving him a coaching role with the younger players, although there was also talk of the FA courting him.

Wright had been joined on England's 1959 early-summer tour by Peter Broadbent, Ron Flowers and Norman Deeley, the latter winning his only two senior caps on a trip that took the players to the Americas, where they lost 2-0 to Brazil in Rio de Janeiro and 4-1 to Peru in Lima before, on the way home, losing in Mexico and crushing the Americans 8-1.

"The crowd in Brazil was about 120,000 and the guards carried guns to keep them under control," said Deeley of a game in which Wolves players filled all the shirts numbered from five to eight. "Brazil had Pele, Didi and Santos and were the best side I've ever seen. They showed why they were world champions. But we had played about 60 matches, it was red-hot and the pitch was hard. We were used to rain and snow! The game in Peru was Jimmy Greaves' debut and he scored - as he always seemed to on his debut."

Broadbent played in only the first match and Deeley in the first two but Flowers started three and went on as a substitute in Mexico City, scoring twice in the much less arduous task against the USA in Los Angeles four days later and starting to make himself an international regular. That last game emerged as Wright's final competitive one before retirement and, back on home soil, the club captaincy was passed, not surprisingly, to Eddie Stuart.

The South African once lived in digs near to where his skipper lodged with the Colley family just outside Tettenhall, and said: "I used to travel to games and training with Billy because, as England skipper, he could get on the bus for free! I was his vice-captain for five or six years and we became very close friends. I was naturally thrilled to be named as his successor."

It was barely a week before Stuart got his hands on some silverware. The Charity Shield had been brought forward to the start of a season as an experiment and Wolves won it outright for the first time as they hit back from one down to beat Nottingham Forest 3-1 at Molineux. Then Bobby Mason, who had started 1958-59 with a hat-trick against Forest, launched their latest title defence with the winner at Birmingham.

Wolves were soon among the goals in a big way, Jimmy Murray leading from the front with braces at home and away against Sheffield Wednesday and Deeley

George Showell (left) looks on in Wolves' opening-day victory at Birmingham. The defender had an awesome act to follow.

Tiny Norman Deeley at large in a 3-3 draw with Arsenal - a game he scored twice in.

having a purple patch with two equalisers in a draw at Arsenal and scoring in five successive September games. The most eye-catching result, though, was a 6-4 away win over Manchester City, where Murray and Bill Slater were both on target twice and Billy McAdams hit a hat-trick for the losers, who were two up in seven minutes.

The champions lost for the first time in a club record 20 matches when they failed to perform at Fulham - then they were then clapped off by the Londoners after exacting

Danger - and a shock - for Wolves on their midweek visit to Fulham in September, 1959. It was their first defeat of the campaign.

ample Molineux revenge to the tune of 9-0 only a week later. Deeley scored four on a night when Wolves hit five in 15 second-half minutes to go second, the winger adding two more in a 5-1 romp at Luton after reverting to no 7 from the left-wing role he had filled for several months.

Deeley, whose posting at no 11 had allowed Micky Lill to be accommodated on the right, bagged 12 goals in six weeks but then didn't add to his League tally for nearly five months in which

No 6 Eddie Clamp turns his head to watch Eddie Stuart clear Wolves' lines during their first-leg European Cup defeat away to Vorwaerts.

Wolves' second sortie into the European Cup started disappointingly. Broadbent's early goal wasn't enough to stave off a 2-1 defeat against Vorwaerts in Berlin, where Stuart was hurt and stretchered off.

Wolves hit the bar and post five times in front of a 55,000-plus audience but outplayed the champions of East Germany at Molineux to edge through by the odd goal, only to then suffer again themselves as Bobby Smith scored

OFFICIAL SOUVENIR PROGRAMME

CELTIC v. WOLVERHAMPTON WANDERERS
(English League Champions)

It's a goal! And it is always a moment of supreme joy when the ball flashes into the opponents' goal. The feeling of elation is caught in this flash-back photograph of our forwards completing an assault by sending the leather into the net.

FIRST FLOODLIT MATCH AT CELTIC PARK
MONDAY, 12TH OCTOBER, 1959 — KICK-OFF 7.15 P.M.

PRICE **6**D.

Colin Booth is out of luck with this effort in a 5-1 crash in front of a 59,344 crowd at Tottenham. Left: The souvenir Celtic programme that described Wolves as the most accomplished side in Europe.

four of the five by which leaders Tottenham thrashed them. Billy Wright was in a massive White Hart Lane crowd to see his old team for the first time since his departure, ironically on the day Showell was absent for the first time in 1959-60.

Two nights later, Wolves were in Glasgow for a friendly to mark the switching-on of Celtic's new floodlights. It was a reciprocal visit for when the Scots had become the first major British club to play under the Molineux lights and was a happy one for Malcolm Finlayson, the keeper who had just completed his first century of Wanderers appearances after being rejected at Parkhead as a 15-year-old.

"Unfortunately, we ruined the night for them by winning 2-0," he recalls. "I was the only Scot in the Wolves side but didn't get the warmest of receptions. I couldn't wear my normal green jersey because of the clash with Celtic's colours and Joe Gardiner offered me the choice of red and blue. I opted for blue, which didn't go down too well because the home fans soon reminded me it was the colour associated with their arch rivals, Rangers!"

Wednesbury-born John Kirkham, given his first senior game at Parkhead, was retained for a League debut the following weekend at home to none other than Manchester United. Right-back Phil Kelly also kept his place because of Showell's injury and, with Cliff Durandt in as well, there was a young look to a side who moved level on points at the top with a thrilling 3-2 win.

From left, Peter Broadbent, Jimmy Murray and Norman Deeley lead the charge on Manchester United's goal in an exciting 3-2 Wolves win on October 17, 1959. Wolves, for whom Murray scored twice and Broadbent once, led 3-0 at one stage.

It was subsequently announced that Wright was moving home with his wife Joy to London - the strongest signal yet that he wouldn't be taking up a fresh post on the Molineux payroll after all. With Stuart filling in at centre-half, though, for the first time since 1951-52, Wolves might have longed to see those blond locks again as they continued to leak goals, Preston beating them 4-3 at Deepdale despite a Des Horne brace.

Scoring was not a problem for Cullis' men. They had 43 goals to their name from 14 League matches, which was why the manager felt able to sell Colin Booth to Nottingham Forest after two weeks' deliberation by the player. Booth, a member of the 1952-53 FA Youth Cup final side, also interested Birmingham as he struggled to command a first-team place at Molineux.

In the wake of his departure, Wolves saw off visiting Newcastle with two goals in the first two minutes, only to then catch a cold at Burnley in the first week of November. Eddie Clamp was recalled at Turf Moor, where he had also played in the reserves the previous Saturday, but a Bobby Mason equaliser was the only highlight in an unhappy 4-1 defeat, the repercussions of which would not be felt in full until some six months later…..

Cullis missed the game as he was in London ready to go spying on Wolves' next European Cup opponents, Red Star Belgrade, in a league match in Titograd. To his annoyance, he was fog-bound at the airport and didn't make it past standing on the terraces, in disguise, at one of the day's First Division fixtures! He wasn't the only member of the party to hit problems, either. Wolverhampton's mayor flew with the party and lost his case en route.

An unusual slant on the teams for the tie in Belgrade, as listed in Red Star Programme.

Eyes fixed on the ball ...Ron Flowers during Wolves' emphatic win at Luton in October, 1959.

Wolves were the first English club to face Red Star away since the tragic Manchester United trip in 1958 and were facing a side holding four cups in effect, having won their domestic KO twice in 1958-59 due to the previous year's final being held over to increase preparation time for the Sweden World Cup.

Showell was back for the first time since the home leg against Vorwaerts and was part of a team who were criticised in the Yugoslav press for rough-house tactics. Wolves were able to brush the brickbats aside as sour grapes, though, satisfied as they were with the 1-1 draw secured by Deeley's headed goal.

Mason scored twice to help defeat Leeds in front of Molineux's smallest crowd of the season, 21,546, and netted again in a defeat at West Ham, who prevailed thanks to a John Dick hat-trick. The Hammers were emerging as a bogey team to Wolves but had become a tough nut for many sides to crack, having won at Arsenal in their previous game to become the new First Division leaders.

Wolves had lost four successive away League games and been beaten in six out of seven First Division trips. But Red Star discovered how formidable they still were at home as they were overpowered in the European Cup return, Murray's centre-cum-shot and Mason's late brace doing the trick in front of 55,519. Finlayson was happy with his clean sheet after his error brought the Yugoslavs' goal in the away leg.

Chelsea were then sent packing from Molineux as Flowers dug deep into his stamina reserves, scoring twice despite adding two midweek England games to a workload already intensified by Wolves' European commitments. Clamp netted the other against the Londoners as Slater, realising he had a major battle to get in at wing-half, played at centre-half for the first time.

Cullis did some extra travelling of his own when going to Glasgow to tie up the £12,500 purchase of Kilmarnock's Joe McBride. Alas, this was one signing that didn't work out. The forward failed to progress beyond the Molineux reserve side and would not make a single first-team appearance before being moved on again.

Criticism had grown of Wolves' physical approach - maybe born out of the jealousy that so often comes from a highly successful side - but skipper Stuart felt compelled to complain to the PFA after Manchester United's Dennis Viollet had been particularly scathing in a newspaper article.

The side needed to be competitive to wear Albion down on December 5, when a header from

Murray 12 minutes from the end proved the only goal of the game. No sooner had they put an end to their poor away sequence, though, than they surrendered their tremendous record of going 20 home matches undefeated in all competitions. Supposedly refreshed following a three-day break in Blackpool, Wolves lost 3-0 to a Leicester side who started the day in 20th place and who had former Molineux reserve Tommy McDonald as their first scorer.

The shock defeat was one of three in four games, a post-Christmas double at the hands of bogey club Bolton following the usual home victory over Birmingham, which was missed by Flowers because of the death of his father and by Broadbent through illness. In their absence, Wolves had the all-Springbok partnership of Durandt and Horne on the left flank while Mason scored twice to join Murray and Deeley with goal totals in the teens.

There was still an excited buzz around the club, magnified when the European Cup draw was made in Paris. Wolves were paired with Barcelona, who already had to find room in their busy schedule to arrange an Inter Cities Fairs Cup final against Birmingham. In the same week that they learned they would be playing in the redeveloped 100,000-seater Nou Camp Stadium, Cullis' men were handed a tough FA Cup trip to Newcastle.

The home game against Bolton was Murray's 150th in the League and another landmark was recorded when Finlayson extended his sequence of successive First Division appearances to 50 in a spectacular 4-4 draw at Arsenal. That January 2 thriller, marked by a last-gasp Gunners equaliser from a penalty, meant Wolves were unbeaten in seven trips to Highbury.

It wasn't unusual for the gates to be closed at 1.30 when the champions were in town and over 62,000 were at their Cup tie at Newcastle a week after close on 48,000 had seen them at Arsenal.

St James' Park was a full seven-hour coach trip away in those days, so two Dakota planes were chartered to whisk more than 70 of Wolves' more affluent fans to the tie.

More than 110,000 fans turned out in total for Wolves' trips to Arsenal in the League and to Newcastle in the Cup as the club's sights stayed fixed on the big prizes. Above: An escape for Wanderers in the blockbuster at Highbury. Right: Peter Broadbent's shot at St James'.

"Newcastle always seemed to reach the final or thereabouts at that time and we joked that their fans probably had their coaches booked for Wembley already," Finlayson said. In the event, it was very much cut and thrust, with a Flowers special and Clamp penalty giving a 2-1 half-time lead to a Wolves side for whom the superb Slater was preferred at centre-half to Showell. But George Eastham had the last say in a 2-2 draw.

Cullis described the subsequent home draw against Second Division Charlton as a 'tremendous spur' to win the replay. And win it they did in the Molineux snow, another long-range Flowers goal contributing to a 4-2 win that Wolves replicated in the League at home to Manchester City three days later, Broadbent netting twice in the latest scoring spree between the sides.

The increasingly commanding Slater had taken over as skipper against Arsenal and City, then kept things tight at the back as Wolves needed a late own goal from Matt Woods to bring them full points away to languishing Blackburn, whose team contained Derek Dougan. It was the unfortunate no 5's second winner by such means in the fixture in successive seasons.

John Kirkham, playing his second senior game, replaced the unwell Flowers at Ewood Park at a time when Spurs led the table but another new face eluded Wolves when negotiations with Leeds (managed by ex-Wolves defender Jack Taylor) over ex-Scotland schoolboy international forward Chris Crowe broke down.

Wolverhampton Wanderers v Barcelona at Molineux in the 1959-60 European Cup. Bill Slater meets his counterpart.

It became four victories in a row as Charlton were despatched from the FA Cup in thick mud at Molineux, though the Second Division Londoners, galvanised by a week's training in Weston-Super-Mare, took an early lead and battled hard.

Billy Wright, six months on from his retirement, returned to Molineux to follow Jimmy Mullen as only the second Wolves player to receive £1,000 as a third benefit payment. The handover came at the visit of Blackpool, who enhanced their status as one of the country's most attractive sides by helping pull in 36,347 after four League gates in a row of under 30,000.

Stan Matthews returned to action at 45 after an injury absence of two and a half months and the 1-1 draw was followed by more nostalgia, Wright being asked along by Wolves as a special guest for their European Cup trip to Barcelona.

With Slater unable to be released from his Birmingham University duties, Stuart was named for the Nou Camp after being in and out of the side for several weeks. He

Peter Broadbent, watched by Jimmy Murray and no 11 Norman Deeley, goes close to his second goal in Wolves' FA Cup fifth-round success at Leicester.

bravely predicted that Wolves were capable of 'at least a draw' while Barca manager Helenio Herrera demanded a three-goal cushion as the return would be played 'in foggy, cold weather on a wet field in front of a fanatical crowd.'

Stereotypes or not, Wolves, having asked their wartime guest player Emilio Aldecoa along as an interpreter, were in front of the largest attendance they had seen since the 1949 FA Cup final, the 95,000 crowd delighting in seeing them outclassed. The 4-0 beating, in which Finlayson suffered a shoulder injury when colliding with a post early on, virtually extinguished Molineux hopes of further progress.

Finlayson's run of 64 consecutive first-team appearances ended there, Geoff Sidebottom taking over as the title pursuit was resumed impressively with a Murray brace in a win at Everton. The reserve keeper, lined up as the 'swap' in the aborted Chris Crowe deal, kept his place in the Luton game on February 20 - in the FA Cup at muddy Kenilworth Road, though, rather than in the League in the West Midlands as originally decreed by the fixture planners.

Luton were bottom of the table but were harshly represented by a 4-1 defeat that was built on Mason's two goals. And their efforts in the rearranged Division One clash of the clubs at Molineux three days later ended in a narrow defeat that left Wolves second at the 30-game stage, one point behind Spurs and two clear of third-placed Burnley. Broadbent hit the 88th minute decider, then laughed off reports that he was soon to retire at the age of 26!

Horne was also on target in the completion of a seasonal treble over the Hatters and was having a terrific 1959-60. He had been training as a fitter and turner in a Durban power station barely three years earlier but had progressed to such an extent that Cullis felt able to sell fellow winger Micky Lill to Everton for £20,000. But that Luton game was not as happy for another Wolves-based South African.

Stuart had missed only seven games in two and a half seasons up to January 1, then apartheid-related events back home, particularly the police's slaying of nearly 60 protestors in the black township of Sharpeville cost him his place for a lengthy spell.

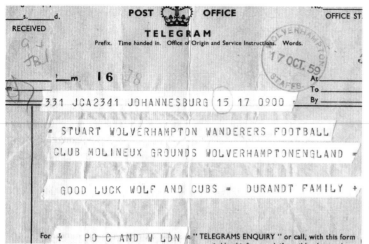

POST OFFICE
TELEGRAM
Prefix. Time handed in. Office of Origin and Service Instructions. Words.

16

331 JCA2341 JOHANNESBURG 15 17 0900

= STUART WOLVERHAMPTON WANDERERS FOOTBALL

CLUB MOLINEUX GROUNDS WOLVERHAMPTONENGLAND =

GOOD LUCK WOLF AND CUBS = DURANDT FAMILY +

For + PO C AND W LDN e " TELEGRAMS ENQUIRY " or call, with this form

Message of a happier kind for Eddie Stuart - from the Durandts.

"We had a general store situated on Newhampton Road and I started getting letters about the atrocities," Stuart says. "Some were supportive but others were very unpleasant. When I led Wolves out against Luton, there was some booing even from our fans. It hurt a lot because, like all decent people, I utterly deplored what was happening in South Africa. I was a Christian and used to pray before meals as well as take a Sunday school class in Perton when I first arrived.

"I was never a racist and often spoke out against those who were. I also think Nelson Mandela is the greatest man of all time. I was going to do a radio show on one of my visits back to Johannesburg a few years ago and was so disappointed when a chance to meet him fell through. Cynthia, my wife, was in tears about the letters. Stan was upset as well. We spoke on the Monday and he decided to rest me."

Stuart lost his full-back place to Showell as the latter moved from centre-half, and the captaincy passed to Slater. But it wasn't until May that Stuart discovered how expensive his axeing was. In his absence, Wolves roared on towards the title when three goals in the first 23 minutes completed the double over an Albion side who, like themselves, had been unbeaten in the League in 1960.

Showell's wife presented him with a son the day before the Barcelona return but that's where the good news ended, Wolves, needing a comeback of 1958 FA Youth Cup final proportions, being hammered 5-2. Sandor Kocsis, one of the survivors of Honved's famous visit to Molineux, scored four and the gulf made it England v Hungary all over again.

It was the first time Wolves had lost to foreign opponents under their floodlights and Cullis said: "If we had to be beaten, I'm glad it was by a side like this. They were magnificent in every aspect of the game." With Manchester United losing 6-1 to Real Madrid the previous October, the standard of English football was once again under the miscroscope....

By coincidence, United were Wolves' next opponents and Major Frank Buckley - handwriting his memoirs in his Walsall flat after hitting on hard times at nearly 80 - would have applauded Cullis' team selection. Young forwards Gerry Mannion and Barry Stobart were handed League debuts, the latter heading the killer goal in a 2-0 win and his 19-year-old colleague making both.

A foot injury kept Murray out at Old Trafford and halted his run of 59 successive appearances and he was again absent when Wolves travelled on FA Cup quarter-final day to take on Albion's fifth-round conquerors, Leicester. Wolves had met the East Midlanders twice in the competition - in the 1949 final and in 1938-39, when they reached the final - so the omens were good.

The double was very much 'on' - reflected by the status of 7-2 Cup favourites - and Cullis, whose team had done relatively little on the knockout front in the previous ten years, argued: "If we win the Cup, nobody can say we didn't deserve to after three away draws in four."

Stobart, but not Mannion, was retained at Filbert Street, where the 10,000 away following were cheered as Gordon Banks was beaten by Broadbent and his own skipper Len Chalmers in the opening 23 minutes. Tommy McDonald scored against his old club for the second time in the season but Wolves won 2-1 and were paired with Second Division Aston Villa in the semi-final.

"This was the one draw I did not want," said Villa boss Joe Mercer. "It would have been so much better as the final!" Cullis promptly took his entire squad to watch Villa's win from two down at home to Derby then Mercer had his players in the Molineux stand the following night as Wolves conceded twice in the last 12 minutes to draw 3-3 with Preston.

Kirkham, Mannion and Stobart again filled in against North End, the latter scoring in a game highlighted by two Broadbent gems. But Clamp skied a penalty 'towards Bushbury,' in the words of Commentator in the Express & Star and Wolves squandered more vital League points when losing on a quick return to Filbert Street, where the fit-again Murray scored while playing for the first time in more than two years at inside-forward - considered by many to be his best position.

In Horne's injury absence, Deeley was back on the left wing, where he had scored ten times in ten matches in a blistering start to the season. The goals had since dried up for him but, as 20,000 Wolves fans queued at Molineux for tickets for the Hawthorns semi-final, he could have been excused for wondering whether his career might have taken a different course.

"I used to play football for an hour and a half at the local playing fields after school," he said. "My Dad came over this one day and told me that Albion wanted me for a trial. I only got on for the second half, though, and then I hurt my knee after a minute or two and was carried off. That was that. I ended up at Wolves instead."

The 'semi' meant a reunion with Nigel Sims, the keeper who had left Wolves in 1956 because of his limited first-team opportunities. It also sparked good-natured banter. Deeley added: "I met Simsy in Lester's clothes shop in Wolverhampton the day before the game and he said we wouldn't score past him because we were too small. I had a go back at him - all in good part, of course!"

The countdown was a stressful one for Finlayson despite his successful return in the second string. "Geoff Sidebottom went in for me and did well," he says. "He played in the fifth and sixth rounds and I knew that if I didn't play against Villa, I wouldn't play in the final if we got through. The strange thing was that Nigel Sims had a similar injury at the same time and neither of us wanted to let on in case we got extra shoulder charges!"

Finlayson made it but Deeley soon joined the

Malcolm Finlayson dives out to deny Gerry Hitchens in Wolves' 1-0 FA Cup semi-final victory over Aston Villa at The Hawthorns.

casualty list when he hurt his groin at The Hawthorns - after he had scored with a volley when Murray's shot was pushed out. "There were no substitutes, so I stayed on the left-wing and was marked by Stan Lynn," he said. "We won comfortably enough, although it was only 1-0, and I had manipulation straight afterwards to try to make sure I was fit for the final."

Wolves, safely through to Wembley for the first time in 11 years and in their eighth FA Cup final, were further cheered by events elsewhere. Blackburn, over whom they had done a League double that season, beat Sheffield Wednesday - 12 places higher in the table come May - in the other semi-final. But the destiny of the title would be sorted out in the meantime.

Cullis' men took a huge step in the right direction when they avenged their Turf Moor hiding

with a 6-1 annihilation of Burnley, right-winger Mannion netting twice on a day all the forwards scored and going one better with all the goals in the win at Leeds three days later.

The former England youth international's purple patch continued when he struck again in a 5-0 slaughter of West Ham, Murray scoring twice to take his League tally past 25, only for Wolves to then lose at Newcastle. The champions remained well placed to retain their crown, though, by taking three Easter points out of four against Nottingham Forest, who missed a penalty in the 0-0 City Ground draw.

Wolves were now three points clear with two matches to go but Burnley had two games in hand. And Tottenham, level with the Lancashire club, threw a spanner in the Molineux works with a 3-1 win away to Cullis' men in front

Burnley's goal comes under threat in their 6-1 hiding at Molineux. Below: Colin Booth, third from left and by now in Forest strip, sees keeper Finlayson gather safely.

of a huge 56,283 crowd on the penultimate Saturday. The pendulum had swung again - and it had swung decisively against the champions.

They rose brilliantly to the challenge on the last

afternoon, though, when running amok with a 5-1 victory at lowly Chelsea, an outstanding all-round performance being highlighted by the two Horne goals that made him the sixth Wanderers player to reach double figures. Now it was all up to Burnley to show their mettle.

With a Wembley final to look forward to and hopes of a third League title still alive, Wolves were in great spirits as they left Stamford Bridge, so much so that Malcolm Finlayson ribbed Chelsea's Peter Sillett, a former colleague of his in the RAF, by telling

Malcolm Finlayson sees a Chelsea effort safely outside his post at Stamford Bridge on the day Wolves hit top form to keep alive their hopes of an historic League and Cup double.

him: "You're the lucky one. You can go off and have a good summer's rest now. We've still got an important match to prepare for and play."

But Molineux dreams of recording the country's first League and Cup double since Villa in 1897 disappeared two days later in yet another scenario that wouldn't be allowed to unfold now. Burnley had one match left, a rearranged one at Manchester City, and won it 2-1, with an agitated Cullis in the crowd. "We were shattered to miss out on the League title but felt we lost it when Spurs beat us in our last home game," Finlayson added. "We played really well at Chelsea to stay alive but it didn't quite prove enough."

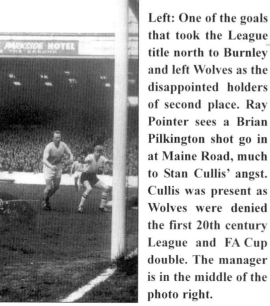

Left: One of the goals that took the League title north to Burnley and left Wolves as the disappointed holders of second place. Ray Pointer sees a Brian Pilkington shot go in at Maine Road, much to Stan Cullis' angst. Cullis was present as Wolves were denied the first 20th century League and FA Cup double. The manager is in the middle of the photo right.

131

Some inevitably reflected on Wright's retirement, wondering whether another season of the master, even ten or a dozen games, might have made the difference. After all, Wolves had conceded 18 more goals than in 1958-59 and Showell had played only half of his 32 League games in his intended centre-half position, the rest coming impressively at right-back.

Tottenham, themselves on the brink of greatness, finished a point behind Wolves, whose 106 First Division goals had taken them comfortably past the century mark for the third successive year. Murray, as in 1957-58 and 1958-59, had topped their League charts, this time with 29, to which he added five in the cups. Broadbent's contribution was 19 and Deeley's was 17 - and unfinished!

The little winger's semi-final injury had cost him his ever-present record but he returned for the last two League matches before Cullis dropped something of a bombshell with his Wembley selection. Tipton-born Mason had played in every round up to the final, in every tie the club had played in the competition for more than three years and in 37 of that season's 42 Division One games. He had also scored 19 goals in 1959-60 but missed the victory at Chelsea, where Stobart excelled for a side who played so well that the manager, in a deviation from his 1949 policy with Jesse Pye and Dennis Wilshaw, said: "Right, that's my Wembley team."

Mason licked his wounds and shunned subsequent efforts to have a special medal struck for him. If he couldn't have the real thing, he didn't want one at all. "We were all upset for Bobby," Deeley said. "He played throughout the run, including the semi-final, but missed the big one."

Deeley may have missed a sizeable chunk of his career to the services but the two goals he scored at Wembley underlined the fact that he hadn't been a bad investment for £10. He attributed his goal-scoring prowess to the countless hours he spent practising in the long-demolished shooting pen beneath the Waterloo Road Stand but, in the wake of his semi-final winner, his participation at Wembley came under threat from a now notorious challenge in the first half of the final.

"Dave Whelan clattered into me and left a lump the size of a duck egg on my shin," he added.

Urgent half-time treatment for Norman Deeley from coach Joe Gardiner. It's just as well the winger played on at Wembley...

"I needed treatment but was not going to come off in a Cup final. It was clear he was in trouble, though, and he was stretchered off with a broken leg. Blackburn being down to ten men probably made it easier for us but it was still a memorable day. It was the only time I'd played on that turf because I stayed on the bench when I was in the party for an England v Italy game."

Mick McGrath's own goal in the 41st minute had just given Wolves the lead when Whelan departed. The full-back failed to fully recover and put the pay-out from his injury misfortune into

Young Barry Stobart, the surprise inclusion in Wolves' FA Cup final line-up, is beaten on this occasion by Blackburn keeper Harry Leyland, with Rovers centre-half Matt Woods also in attendance.

an alternative business career that has led to multi-millionaire status and the compensation of financing Wigan's rise to the Premiership.

In his absence at Wembley, Deeley got down to business, cashing in on fine work by left-winger Horne to score no 2 midway through the second half and making it three with a late shot into the roof of the net after Stobart turned provider for the second time.

Deeley recalls hearing Kenneth Wolstenholme saying it had been a poor game to watch but the criticism didn't sit easily with Finlayson - and still doesn't. "One columnist called it the dustbin final and I think that tag stuck over the years," he said. "But it was 85 degrees out there. It was one of the hottest days I ever remember playing football on, and we had the ball in their net five times, so we couldn't have played too badly. I'm sure it was a better game than we were given credit for."

Slater had played for free when representing Blackpool in the 1951 showpiece and was the last amateur ever to play in the FA Cup final, the programme 54 years ago reflecting his status by calling him W J Slater.

It's difficult to comprehend now but he returned home unrecognised and alone by train straight after the game as he was under a strict curfew from his teacher-training college in

The tension of the Wolves bench at Wembley.

COUNTY BOROUGH ✦ OF WOLVERHAMPTON

CIVIC BANQUET
TO
WOLVERHAMPTON WANDERERS F.C.
Wednesday, 25th May, 1960

Seating Arrangements

IMPORTANT :
ARRANGEMENTS FOR ENTRANCE TO BANQUET HALL.
GUESTS seated at TABLE A to use Doors 2 & 3 (North Promenade)
GUESTS seated at TABLES B — H (inclusive)
to use Doors 4, 5, 6 & 7 (Civic Hall Main Foyer)
GUESTS seated at TABLES J — N (inclusive)
to use Door 1 (North Promenade)
See Plan on last page.

Bill Slater crowns a memorable personal year by getting his hands on the FA Cup in May, 1960. The handover by the Duchess of Gloucester was some consolation for team of the season Wolves for missing out on the League title.

Leeds; alone, that is, apart from dozens of Newcastle fans in the same compartment celebrating their side's 2-0 win in the time-honoured fashion!

He had extra reason to walk tall in 1960. During FA Cup final weekend, he became the first part-timer to win the coveted Footballer of the Year award, although Burnley chairman Bob Lord, a senior FA figure, had said before the awards dinner: "The press have got it wrong this time. It should have gone to (Burnley inside-forward) Jimmy McIlroy."

The modest Slater later recalled: "When I stood up to collect the award, I received the biggest cheer you could imagine. It was a very special moment at the end of three wonderful seasons." Mr Lord's outspoken comments had been put in their place and Cullis had been vindicated for reprimanding his player for setting his sights too low at their first meeting in 1952, when he expressed an interest in having a game in 'one of the Wolves teams.' The Iron Man made it clear he wasn't interested in anyone unless they had ambitions to play first-team football.

Celebration time, with a deserved drink for two-goal Norman Deeley.

Wolves' happy players and their womenfolk in the party mood after all the Wembley formalities.

One of those struggling to take it all in was Barry Stobart. The FA Cup final was only his sixth first-team game and he recalls: "I really felt for Bobby Mason - it must have been a killer for him. I thought I had a chance of playing because I'd done reasonably well at Chelsea the week before but if anyone had told me a fortnight beforehand that I would be playing at Wembley, I'd never have believed them. It was a different world to the one I was used to."

Not so enamoured with the experience was Stuart - the other casualty in addition to Mason. He had lost his place through unfortunate outside influences and missed out at Wembley amid more than a little irony. After all, it was Showell's excellence as a stand-in centre-half that had hastened Wright's departure. Now, with the replacement's form as a first-team regular not as impressive, he had switched positions to full-back dislodge another Wolves skipper.

"I generally preferred playing at centre-half because I usually played better there," Showell now says. "But I had a bad spell in the Cup-winning season and went to right-back again. Of course I had some sympathy for Eddie but that was how competitive things were at Wolves. I'd had to be very patient to win a regular place and, although I never asked for a move, there was once a link with QPR that came to nothing."

As Wolves looked forward to their first crack at the European Cup Winners' Cup, Stuart was left with the regret of never playing in a Wembley final. And the misfortune certainly hurt him. "That business in South Africa couldn't have happened at a worse time," he said. "I had been the youngest player ever to appear in a South African cup final aged 16 and a half, but to play in an English final at Wembley was every young player's dream.

"I would have been the first foreigner to captain a team in the FA Cup final and was absolutely devastated not to be selected. I went to the game, sat on the bench and joined the players at the banquet afterwards. I tried to enjoy it but I couldn't. The disappointment was too great. Thankfully, though, I had a lot more ups than downs because playing at Wolverhampton Wanderers in those days was very, very special."

June, 2005

As Time Rolled By

Bert Williams played 420 League, FA Cup and Charity Shield games for Wolves, plus several dozen prestige 'friendlies' and 30 Football League (South) fixtures. He won 24 England caps and became a highly successful businessman. He was 83 in January, 2005 and still lives in the Midlands.

Eddie Stuart ended a stay of 322 Wolves games by joining Stoke in 1962. He was captain as the Potters returned to the top flight in his first season there, later playing for Tranmere, Stockport and Worcester. He is now retired from a hair salon business and lives in the Midlands.

Roy Pritchard followed his 223 Wolves senior matches by breaking his jaw on his Aston Villa debut against Arsenal in 1956. That set an unfortunate pattern as he played only once in each of his three seasons at Villa before joining Notts County, then Port Vale. He died in January, 1993.

Lawrie Kelly, having guested for Halifax in the war, played nearly 240 games for Huddersfield after his Molineux career of 70 League and Cup games ended in 1950. A Wulfrunian, he then had a stint as Nuneaton manager but died in Aldershot in February, 1979, aged 53.

Nigel Sims won an England B cap while at Wolves but managed only 39 appearances for the club before totalling over 300 outings for Aston Villa, whom he helped win the FA Cup in 1957. He later played for Peterborough and in Toronto, and worked in insurance. He now lives in Wales.

Angus McLean played 158 League and Cup games for Wolves and then became Aberystwyth player-manager in his native Wales in 1951. He was later Bury's trainer and served Crewe before succeeding Brian Clough as Hartlepool boss in 1967. He died in Scotland in July, 1979, aged 53.

Terry Springthorpe's Molineux stay of 38 League and Cup appearances (plus many more in wartime) ended with a move to Coventry in December, 1950. He later played in South Africa and America and, at the age of 81, now lives in the south west of England.

Alf Crook served Wellington and Kidderminster after leaving Wolves in 1950, having been injured in his second game. He worked as a manager in the glass trade and still lives in the Midlands.

Bill Crook took the opposite course to several others by moving to Walsall from Wolves, his 1954 switch leading to 52 Saddlers appearances. He had played more than 220 times for Wolves in peacetime alone and later moved to the north west, where he still lives.

Ray Chatham's 76-game Wolves career ended with a move to Notts County in January, 1954. After 130 games and four years at Meadow Lane, the Wulfrunian headed south east to play for Margate. He then worked in London, having trained as a draughtsman, but died several years ago.

Bill Shorthouse swapped playing for Wolves (after 376 appearances) for coaching them and carved out a fine career in the backroom, going on to work with the England youth team, Aston Villa and Birmingham. He also scouted for Villa in later years and still lives in the Midlands.

Billy Wright never did coach at the club for whom he played 541 League and cup games, plus 117 in the war and countless prestige matches. Instead, the holder of the CBE worked with England youths and under-23s and had a four-year stint as Arsenal boss from 1962, after which he worked for many years in TV. He was made a Wolves director in 1990 and died in September, 1994.

Johnny Hancocks followed his 378 Wolves matches with a stint as player-boss of Wellington Town before serving Cambridge United, Oswestry and GKN Sankey. Working life also took him to RAF Cosford from the same Oakengates street as the one in which he was born. He died in 1994.

Leslie Smith, who scored 24 goals when restricted to 94 games in nine years at Wolves, won an FA Cup winner's medal in his first season at Aston Villa and had 130 outings for them, scoring 25 goals. He retired through serious Achiles damage in 1960 and still lives in his native Midlands.

Jimmy Dunn added 57 League games with Derby to his Wolves peacetime haul of 144 and also played for Worcester City and Runcorn before hanging up his boots in 1959. He then coached at Albion for several years and later became a physio and a publican. He still lives in the Midlands.

Sammy Smyth is back in his native Northern Ireland, where he worked for a bookmaker and had his own sports shop following his football career. Having moved to Stoke in 1951 after 116 appearances while at Molineux, he scored 19 goals in 44 games to earn a move to Liverpool in 1954.

Jesse Pye's fine record of 95 goals in 209 Wolves games brought him England recognition - but only one full cap. He cost Wolves a club record £12,000 from Notts County and later played for Luton, Derby and Wisbech. He then became a hotelier in Blackpool, where he died in 1984 at 64.

Dennis Wilshaw followed his successful Molineux stint by scoring 50 times in over 100 games for his home-city club Stoke, a broken leg at Newcastle ending his career in 1961. He climbed the ladder in the teaching profession and also did some scouting for Stoke. He died in May, 2004.

Jimmy Mullen totalled 486 games and 112 goals in a fabulous 21-year Wolves career that also brought 12 England caps. Like team-mates Ron Flowers and Bert Williams, he ran a successful sports shop in Wolverhampton for many years but died suddenly at a dance in the autumn of 1987.

Dennis Parsons played 27 Wolves League and Cup games as understudy to Bert Williams - plus others in the war - and had a similar fate after joining Aston Villa in 1952 via Hereford. He also played non-League before retiring in 1960. He died in Solihull in 1980 just before his 55th birthday.

Willie Forbes was a Glaswegian who returned to Scotland via Preston and Carlisle after a 1946-49 Wolves career of 75 games and 23 goals in which he made the switch from inside-forward to centre-forward. He died in Chorley in February, 1999, aged 76.

Eddie Russell made 35 first-team appearances for Wolves before joining Middlesbrough in 1951 and then serving Leicester (101 games) and Notts County. He still lives in Cornwall, where he ran a holiday village, and remains a good friend of Sammy Smyth.

Bill Baxter made 47 League and Cup appearances for Wolves as well as a record 224 in their reserves. He then played over 100 games for Villa, where he coached for many years before also managing East Fife in his native Scotland. He died in the early 2000s.

Roy Swinbourne did some refereeing and played part-time football after being forced to retire through injury following 230 Wolves games and 114 goals. But he devoted his best energies to becoming a successful businessman in the tyre industry. A keen golfer, he lives in the Midlands.

Johnny Walker lives in the Home Counties, having settled during 300 games for Reading and 15 years as their reserve-team coach. He scored 26 goals in 44 Wolves matches before moving to Southampton, for whom he hit 48 goals in 172 games. He has also worked for the Royal Mail.

Jack Short played 107 times for Wolves in all competitions before embarking on what became a well-worn path to Stoke, where he played 55 games. He then appeared well over 100 times for Barnsley in his native Yorkshire before retiring in 1960. He died in 1976 when in his late 40s.

Peter Broadbent is now in a Midlands nursing home, having thrilled a generation of Wolves fans with his 497 outings and 145 goals. He also won seven full England caps and later played for Shrewsbury, Aston Villa and Stockport before retiring and running a baby-wear shop in Halesowen.

Len Gibbons was a full-back who had to be content with a modest 29 first-team Wolves games despite spending seven years at Molineux from 1946. He then played in non-League and is thought to have gone abroad to work in subsequent years.

Norman Deeley won two League title medals and two England caps and played a star role in the 1960 FA Cup final. He scored 73 goals in 237 Wolves games before joining Orient in 1962 and then going into non-League. He has since worked for Walsall FC and still lives in the Midlands.

Ken Whitfield played ten senior matches for Wolves but had a year with Manchester City and played almost 200 games for Brighton, followed by a season with Queens Park Rangers. He lived in South Wales and died in 1995.

Brian Birch was an England youth cap who had three games and nine months at Wolves after signing from Manchester United. In a restless career, he had stints in the Phillipines and Sydney.

Bill Guttridge still lives in his native Midlands, where he had seven years as a loyal Molineux reserve while playing only seven first-team games. He then appeared in well over 200 matches for Walsall, whom he also served as a coach.

Ron Flowers has now passed on to his son the running of the Wolverhampton sports shop he managed for many years after a playing career of 512 Wolves matches, 49 England caps and a host of honours. After Molineux, he played for Northampton and Telford, the latter as player-boss.

Bill Slater totalled 339 Wolves games and 12 full England caps before embarking, via a short second spell at Brentford, on a life in sports administration. Already a Birmingham University teacher, he gained a Bachelor of Science degree and was awarded the OBE and CBE. He lives in London.

John Taylor scored once in ten Wolves games, having made his name with 29 Luton goals in 85 games that led to an England B cap. He later played for Notts County and Bradford Park Avenue.

Ron Stockin was an Albion and Walsall amateur before persuading Stan Cullis to buy him in 1952. He played 21 games for Wolves, then joined Cardiff and scored in their 9-1 home defeat by Wolves in 1955. He later played for Grimsby before returning to the Midlands, where he still lives.

Eddie Clamp totalled 241 games in a Molineux stay of more than a decade before a ten-month spell at Arsenal. He then joined Eddie Stuart in helping Stoke back to the top flight, ending a career that brought him four England caps by serving Peterborough and Worcester. He died in 1995.

George Showell finally made exactly 200 League outings for Wolves before joining Bristol City in 1965. Then he went to Wrexham, where he had 18 months as a player and subsequently embarked on a 25-year career in their coaching and physio team. He still lives in Wales.

Tommy McDonald could only rarely dislodge Johnny Hancocks but played 113 League games at Leicester and later served Dunfermline, Raith, Queen of the South and Stirling, winning one B cap for Scotland. He died in Dunfermline in August, 2004, aged 74.

Colin Booth lives on the south coast, having also resided in Stafford, where he worked at the hospital, and Oxford since his playing career wound down at Doncaster and Oxford. He scored 27 goals in 82 Wolves games mainly in the late 1950s before being sold to Nottingham Forest.

Doug Taylor was one of the sufferers in the shadows of Wolves' star forwards and played only three times for the club before joining Walsall (38 games) in 1955 and then going into non-League.

Gwyn Jones is a proud Welshman who turned 70 earlier this year and lives in Anglesey. He played only 22 games in Wolves' first team but he made 160 senior appearances for Bristol Rovers after moving west in August, 1962.

Ron Howells played only nine games for Wolves before moving to Portsmouth, Scunthorpe and Walsall in a career of over 150 games. He was the son of a Welsh rugby union international.

Bobby Mason is now back in his native Midlands, having worked and lived for years on the south coast. He scored 54 goals in a fine Wolves career spanning 173 senior appearances before moving on to Chelmsford, Leyton Orient and Poole. He turns 70 next year.

Jimmy Murray moved to Molineux from Kent and had a terrific Wolves career of 299 games and 166 goals. He then netted 43 times in 70 Manchester City matches before serving Walsall and Telford. He still lives in the Midlands, having worked in the greengrocery and car businesses.

Joe Bonson ended a promising Wolves stay of 12 games and five goals by moving on in 1957. He then scored regularly at Cardiff, Scunthorpe, Doncaster, Newport, Brentford and Lincoln in a career of 132 senior goals. He died a decade and a half ago.

Malcolm Finlayson played 203 games in a wonderful Molineux career after playing a similar number for Millwall, finally retiring in 1963. He then became a highly successful businessman and still works today as he divides his time between the Midlands and his native Scotland.

Gerry Harris still lives in the Midlands and has worked in horticulture and farming since the end of his football career. He played 270 times for Wolves up to 1966 and won four under-23 caps for England before embarking on a much shorter spell with neighbouring Walsall.

Harry Hooper, now 82, lives in Northamptonshire, having set up in business after ending his playing career at Kettering. His Wolves spell of 41 games and 19 goals was followed by 105 games at Birmingham, including the 1960 Fairs Cup final, and 65 in the League for Sunderland.

Pat Neil was a Hampshire-born left-winger and England amateur international who made only four Wolves senior appearances in the mid-1950s before joining Portsmouth for the second time.

Noel Dwyer played only five Wolves first-team games - all in 1957-58 - but totalled 213 throughout a League career that also took in West Ham, Swansea, Plymouth and Charlton. He won 14 Republic of Ireland caps and later became a licensee. He died in his late 50s in 1992.

Jackie Henderson died in his early 70s in the 2004-05 season, having given Wolves fans just a brief glimpse of his talents. He played only nine games at Molineux but topped 200 for Portsmouth and 100 for Arsenal before finishing his career at Fulham. He also won seven full Scottish caps.

Allan Jackson is another who still lives in his native Midlands, having played six first-team games for Wolves before scoring 43 times in 150 League games for Bury and then served Brighton.

Micky Lill had a fine one-in-two goal record in his 34 Wolves appearances after also winning England youth honours. He later joined Everton, Plymouth and Portsmouth before ending his career in South Africa, where he subsequently taught PE near Johannesburg and died in November, 2004.

Cliff Durandt was born in Johannesburg and strengthened Wolves' South African links by playing 49 games for them. He later played for Charlton and for Germiston Callies, the same club as Micky Lill. The father of a successful boxing promoter, he died several years ago.

Des Horne is also from Johannesburg and totalled 52 games and 18 goals for Wolves before amassing 188 League appearances for Blackpool. He returned to South Africa in 1966 and ran an air-conditioning business. He was last known to be living in his home country.

Phil 'Jimmy' Kelly played only 18 senior games for Wolves before appearing in 130-plus for Norwich and winning five Republic of Ireland caps. He settled in Norfolk and was player-boss of Lowestoft. He worked in the concrete and golf complex businesses and is a retired van driver.

Geoff Sidebottom played 35 times for Wolves and 88 for Villa, also serving Scunthorpe, New York Royal Generals and Brighton, the latter as a coach long enough to have a testimonial. He was also a keen cricketer with Penn and later returned to his native Yorkshire.

Gerry Mannion scored seven goals in only 21 senior appearances for Wolves but then played 119 matches for Norwich and finished his career at Chester. He is reported to have died in his native Warrington in June, 1994, aged 54.

Johnny Kirkham was from Wednesbury and in the infancy of his Wolves career during the glory years. But he flourished to total 112 games for the club before moving on to Peterborough, Exeter and Horwich RMI. He won England youth and under-23 honours while at Molineux.

Barry Stobart had the fine record of 22 goals in 54 Wolves games before spending six months at Manchester City. He scored 20 in 53 games for Villa and served Shrewsbury, then took Willenhall to the FA Trophy final as manager. A window cleaner for many years, he still lives in the Midlands.

Ted Farmer looked like becoming a Molineux great as he burst on to the scene with 44 goals in 62 senior games and won two England under-23 caps in the process. But injury cruelly ended his career at 24. He subsequently worked as a licensee and in business, and still lives in the Midlands.

Subscribers

SCROLL OF HONOUR

A
Bob Adams
Marc and Neil Aldridge
Geoff Allman
Douglas Allsop
Peter John Armfield
Eric Asbury
Michael Ashmore
P N Ashton
Matt Ashwood
Lyndon Attwell

B
Fred Baker
John and Evelyn Baker
Ross Baker
Matt Bakewell
Charlie Bamforth
Neil and Sheila Barnes
Robert Frank Bate
John Bates
Andrew Beeston
Leonard Best
Margaret and Vic Bicknell
George Blackhall
Robert Blackhall
Pam and Peter Blakey
Nigel Bond
Ulf Brennmo
Bryan Bridges
Malcolm Brigstock
Neil Brinsdon
Nigel Bristow
Ruth and Tom Buckley
Paul Burden

David Paul Burrows

C
Alfred Camilleri
Don Carman
Charles Cartwright
Frances Cartwright
Shaun Cartwright
Jonathan Chrimes
John Clarke
David Cleveland
Chris Collier
Graham Cook
John Cook
Christopher Cottam
Steven Cox
Malcolm Crockett
Reginald Crook
John A Cross

D
John Dallaway
Joe and Ash Dallow
Brian N Daniels
Kevin Darlington
Harry Davenhill
Colin Davenport
Kenneth Davies
Roy S Davies
The Davies Family
Barnaby Davis
Eric Deakin
Cecil Deans
Jack Deans
Peter Deans

Gisela Degg
Brian and Helen Dennis
Barney Dowler
Christopher Driver
The Dungars
Keith Dunn

E
Kevin Eccleston
Steve English
George Evans
Jack Evans
Keith Evans
Peter Evans
William Henry Evans
Mark, Kate, Matthew Everiss

F
David Farmer
Roger D Fellows
George Flanagan

G
Dan Gaichas
Mr S R Garner
Maurice Gelipter
F D Gilson
John C Godfrey
Colin Gray
Geoff Green
J B Green
Robert H Green
Ken Gregory
Robert Gubbins
Maggie Alice Guest

SCROLL OF HONOUR

H
Alan Hall
Robert L Hamilton
Nigel Harcourt
Carl Harper
Graham Harridence
Antony John Harris
Reg, Amy and Greg Harris
Neil Harrison
John Harvey
David Haytree
Jim Heath
Margaret Hewitt
Niall Hickman
William John Hickman
Guy O S Holland
Harry Holmes
Jay Hooke
Douglas Robert Hooper
Karl Horvath
Phil Hough
Bruce Howes
David Hughes
Peter Hughes
Quentin Hughes
Thomas Henry Hughes
John D Hurd

J
Adam J Jewkes
Mervyn J Jewkes
F W Jones
Graham Jones
Kenneth Jones
K T Jones

Mark K Jones
Peter and George Jones
Stuart P G Jones
Trevor Jones
Les Jordan

K
John Kedward
David Keeling
Brent Kendrick
Brian Key
Dave Kidd

L
John Lalley
John Lansley
Pauline and Shawn R Law
W G Lawley
Derek Lawton
Michael Leng
Boo Lewis
Godfrey Linder
Hannah and Richard Lloyd
John David Lloyd
Duncan Lowe
Peter C Lowe

M
Gwilym Machin
Truls Mansson
Per Magnar Meyer
Iain, Maria McGuinness
Jean Pierre Micallef
Tarcisio Mifsud
Eric Millington

Dick Milton
Karen Milton
Brian Millward
Maurice Monina
D V Morris
F J Morris
Kenneth Munk

N
Geoff Narraway
Antony D J Nicholls
Brian Nicholls
Isaac S Nicholls
Bob Nicholson

O
Les Oakley
Steve Oates (in memory of
Fred Oates)
Alfred Oseland
Keith Alexander Owen
Terry Owers

P
Malcolm F Palmer
Terry Palmer
Jim Parkes
John Parry
Ronald Peacock
Roy George Pearce
Douglas Pearl
John Pearson
David Phillips
Mick Pipe
Robert Poulton

SCROLL OF HONOUR

Steve Powis
Andrew Prescott
Charlie J E Prescott
Peter Price
Russell Price
M A Pritchard
Michael Prosser
John Pryor

R
Matteo and Dale Race
Norman Edward Radford
Mr C A Raison
Andrew Peter Raybould
Mike Redfern
Gordon Terence Reed
Trevor and Callum Reed
Ken Rees
Bill Richardson
Norman W Round
Raymond Rowley
Chris Rowsell
Patrick Rynn

S
Michael Sampson
Peter John Schofield
F Bernard Shaw
Raymond Noah Sheldon
Ben Sherriff
Carys and Max Sidbotham
George Sinagra
John Skelton
Dave Slape
Mike Slater

Andy Smith
John Smith
Patrick J Smith
Southport Wolf
John Stanford
Peter Starkey
Margaret and Jean Stokes
Jake St Ruth
Christopher Swatman

T
Jonathan L Taylor
Malcolm Spudy Taylor
John B Tew
John Edward Tilley
Jon Tomkins
Graham Tonks
Glyn Tunney, Emma Evans
Tony Turpin

V
George Voulgaris

W
Sam Wadey
In memory of Edward
Wakeley
Graham Walters
Mr S A Walters
Dave Warren
Simon Mark Webb
George Webster
Andrew George Wells
Steven Wells
Dennis Weston

Kenneth Westwood
Mike and Hazel Westwood
Bethany and Jazlin White
Fred Whitehouse
Tony Wild
Joan and Peter Williams
John Williams
Judith A Williams
Alan John Winmill
Mr J Withers
Don Wolvey
Harry Woodman
W D Worrall
Andrew L M Wright
Michael Wright
Michael Wynniatt

Y
Amila Y'Mech
Cyril Young